How to be a
RAPID READER

6 Steps to Increased Speed and Concentration

KATHRYN REDWAY

National Textbook Company
a division of *NTC Publishing Group* • Lincolnwood, Illinois USA

To
Peter and Michael Duncan

This edition first published in 1991 by National Textbook Company,
a divison of NTC Publishing Group, 4255 West Touhy Avenue, Lincolnwood (Chicago), Illinois 60646-1975 U.S.A.
Manufactured in the United States of America.
Library of Congress Catalog Card Number: 90-62788

1 2 3 4 5 6 7 8 9 VP 9 8 7 6 5 4 3 2 1

Acknowledgments

I wish to express my thanks to:

- Tony Buzan and Brian Helweg-Larsen, who introduced me to the subject and guided me in my early days with it

- Cristina Stuart, who suggested I write this book

- Alison Leach, whose friendship, encouragement, and comments were invaluable when I started it

- Susan Mosely Harris, whose experience and comments were particularly helpful

- Norman Duncan for taking the time to sharpen my style and for inspiring my enthusiasm in this and other areas

- Peter Bruggen for his unfailing support for my work

- All my students who taught me to listen and inspired much of the contents of this book

And, of course, Keith, my husband, whose patience, support, and suggestions made me finish the book.

None of these people is responsible for any errors of fact or interpretation in this book.

The author and publishers also wish to thank the following publishers, authors, and agents for permission to reprint copyright material:

Agenzia Letteraria Internazionale for an extract from *The Europeans* by Luigi Barzini; "Talking Tough" by Howard

Banks, reprinted by permission of *Forbes* magazine, July 23, 1990, © Forbes Inc., 1990; *The Times Newspapers Ltd.* for the article "Pöhl walks tightrope of German consensus" from the June 25, 1987, issue; James Edmonds for his article "Time-sharing—The Club/Trustee System;" and A. K. Redway for his article "Management Tools—Project Planning Procedures."

Contents

Introduction

Why Read This Book?

YOU . . . . have picked up . . .

THIS BOOK . . . . to flip through it, to see if it is worth reading or buying.

RAPID READING . . . . is . . .

SIMILAR . . . . to the actions you carry out to determine if you want . . .

TO BUY . . . . or read this book now.

GLANCE . . . . at and understand the . . .

TITLE, ... cover illustration, the . . .

TABLE OF CONTENTS
. . . and chapter headings. Flip through the book to see illustrations and layout, and read through one or two paragraphs. The approach to reading and memorizing described in this book is similar to the process you have just completed. By looking down the left-hand column above you have skimmed the . . .

KEYWORDS . . . . to assess the value of the book to you. You have done your . . .

FIRST RAPID READ.

The purpose of this book is to enable professionals and others, such as students, to assimilate quickly and use documents such as magazines and textbooks more effectively. Many of us have a lot of literature—papers and professional or official documents—to deal with and information to absorb and re-

1

call. By learning to read rapidly, you can increase (typically tenfold) your effectiveness in dealing with documents and the information they contain.

The aim of this book is to boost your confidence and build on what you already know. It gives you a flexible technique that you can adapt to *your* needs.

This book is based on the attitudes and comments of many businesspeople and students who have attended the author's courses. The questions they have raised, the difficulties as well as the enthusiasm have been recorded. This book should often mirror your own thoughts and respond to them.

How to Use This Book

Rapid reading is not just reading faster; it is also the technique of focusing on what you need. The approach of this book is to emphasize the importance of **setting objectives before** you start reading. Identify now what you need most and go to the sections of the book that supply your needs. You do not have to follow this book—or any other textbook—sequentially from page 1 to the end.

A key part of rapid reading lies in the selection of what you need from a document. Things you already know or that are of no interest or use to you must be ignored. This means that rapid reading consists of learning **where** to find information and **how to interpret it.** Many documents contain information you may not need now, but may want to refer to later.

Use this book in the same manner that you use any other document:

- Do you want to find out what it contains?
- Do you want to summarize the contents?

■ Do you want to learn a part of the contents?

If, after your first search through the book, you decide that you need more, go back, but only after you have completed your initial rapid read.

Also, remember that if you enjoy what you are doing, reading will be much more effective.

Who Should Read This Book?

The average professional person with 1.8 children reads four novels and two professional books per year, and each month reads thoroughly one professional magazine and skims (ineffectively) through two other journals connected with his or her work. All this reading occupies, perhaps, one hundred hours per year. This book enables you either to cut this reading time to ten hours per year, with more effective selection of information, retention, and recall, or to read about ten times as much in the same amount of time.

This book is also for people who read few books, because they are discouraged even before they start. To them, many books appear long and, if they are not well presented, intimidating. Many of these readers start on page 1 and laboriously plod through page after page, taking a long time, while others give up early and set a pattern of never finishing a book. For all readers there is a better and quicker way to go about the process.

Differences Between Readers: Professionals and Students

Many adult professionals and students use the same reading methods but are dissatisfied with the results. The dissatisfaction stems from the fact that they are still using the method that they learned **as children.** They do not appreciate that their present purpose in reading is totally different from their reading requirements when they were young and that they should, therefore, be using different reading techniques from those they learned originally.

Students are required to learn certain subjects (for example, economics, law, biology, or accounting) practically by heart. Missing just one word in a test may give the student poor grades. Consequently, these students read with the sole purpose of learning by rote; often they do not comprehend what they are learning.

Professionals, on the other hand, read because they are interested in a report, or because material has piled up in the intray, or because they have to prepare quickly for a meeting. Whatever the reason, no one is going to ask, word for word, what they have read. Thus, their reading method and degree of comprehension should be more flexible.

CHAPTER ONE

What Is Reading?

In this chapter . . .

Rapid reading is a skill. Your success in mastering the skill depends on your attitude, your enthusiasm, and your readiness to try a technique. You must:

■ Want to improve.

■ Be confident that you will do so.

The myths surrounding the reading process are discussed and the reasons why you must abandon them are explained. The facts are that:

■ Reading for both pleasure and work can be fast.

■ Rereading is not necessary to aid comprehension.

■ Reading can be fun and variable.

■ Skimming can be reading.

■ Technical documents can be read rapidly.

■ You do not need to try to remember everything you read.

This chapter describes how the brain is used as you read and how the proper use of both the left and right hemispheres of the brain facilitates rapid reading. By means of a simple exercise, you can determine your initial reading speed and the extent of your comprehension. Then, after learning why comprehension is subjective and how bad habits—such as subvocalizing and lack of concentration—can be changed, you will be taken (in following chapters) through a short sequence of exercises designed to increase your reading speed.

Reading Is an Attitude

This book will give you a systematic approach to improving your reading. But if you are not committed to improvement and do not have a strong belief in your ability to improve, the technique will not work. You must have two things:

■ The wish to improve. This can only come from you. You may wish to improve because you are a slow reader and you want to read more, or because you *must* read, yet you find it difficult to be interested in the material.

■ A confident attitude. Knowing that you want to improve *and* believing that you can, you must simply trust yourself and the advice and information given in this book.

Part of a positive mental attitude—the desire to improve—requires you to be optimistic. Accept that learning to read faster is a process of highs and lows. Each step contains an essential element that contributes to acquiring the technique. Do not look for difficulties **before** you start. Do not analyze each step **until** you have completed it.

First, admit that you must change your habits if you want to read faster. You do not yet know how: that's what this book will tell you. Remember, suspend judgment until you have given the technique a fair trial.

Embarking on something new is an opportunity to extend your knowledge. It will be easier if you can relax and have fun as you go along. This skill makes the same demands on the learner as acquiring any other new skill, say skiing. Be childlike in your attitude. Children quickly sense the exhilaration of other children who can already ski. Their sole objective is to be able to enjoy themselves in the same way. They learn quickly because that objective is always before them. They accept short-term setbacks, like falling over, and they do not question the instructions. Being childlike is being unafraid to make mistakes, it is finding out what works and what does not work. Today you are on the nursery slopes, with a limited speed. Look to the top of the mountain and be determined that you, too, will enjoy the thrill of speed.

Getting Rid of Myths

There are many myths surrounding the reading process. Here are a few:

1. **A good pleasure-read and thorough work reading have to be slow.**

   There is no evidence to support this view. Slow readers, in fact, find pleasure reading too time-consuming to be enjoyable. This, of course, makes such readers reluctant even to start. Slow reading discourages readers because there are so few early rewards. Slow readers get a fragmented comprehension. They miss the overall driving idea and meaning of the material, in the same way a typist who necessarily reads every word may not take in what is typed. The typist's mind wanders off because reading is at the pace of typing—slow and dull. But fast reading, as explained in this book, will prove pleasant for leisure reading and effective for work reading.

2. **When you fail to comprehend or lose concentration, immediately reread.**

   This is one of the most common faults of poor readers—going back to check what they have just read to try to gain understanding. It is very inefficient. It slows them down. It allows their minds to wander off. It sidetracks them from anticipating what is coming. It distracts them from thinking actively.

   A simple technique for increasing comprehension and concentration is to maintain a dialogue with the author. Question the author: why did he or she say that? Is it different from what was said before? Anticipate what the author will say in the next section of the document.

3. **Reading is boring.**

   This myth is popular with those who believe in myths 1 and 2. Reading is fun and rewarding if you are motivated, follow a rhythm, and actively seek information. Reading fast, understanding it, and retaining what is read is even more exciting.

4. **Skimming can't be reading.**

Skimming *is* reading. It is *the* technique to apply when you are looking for something specific and you want to overview a whole document. Skimming is taking mental note of the presentation of material, picking up what stands out, and reading headings and keywords. It is a vital part of rapid reading, sometimes used by itself, but more often in conjunction with other steps. (See Chapters 3 and 4.)

When you learn a new language, you are forced to skim. You grasp only a few words per sentence. Yet you persevere and your perseverance is rewarded. Little by little, you understand more. Apply the same technique when reading.

5. **You need long periods of time to read.**

You don't. If you know how to skim, you can pick up ideas from any document, effectively, in five minutes. But efficient and rapid reading requires concentration. You need to concentrate as soon as you decide to read. When you know what your objectives are, reading can be done in five- or fifteen-minute slots. Long periods spent reading are certainly not synonymous with efficient reading.

6. **Technical documents can't be read rapidly.**

Such documents lend themselves very well to rapid reading. In most cases these documents give background information that the reader does not need, at least to begin with.

Rapid reading is a series of steps. The key step, in the case of technical reports, is to decide beforehand what you are seeking. Then you skim for this material, skimming more carefully when you locate important passages. Of course, because there will be more solid material in such documents than in a novel, the speed used to read the chosen material will be slower than that for a novel. To master the skill of speed reading is to master flexibility—that is, to use different speeds for different materials.

7. **Rapid reading everything will be boring.**

Not so. Rapid reading involves a great variety of approaches that keep reading dynamic and challenging. You adjust your speed according to the material and your purpose in reading it.

8. **When you read you need to remember everything.**

That might have been true at school, but not any more. Read the section of this book entitled "Differences Between Readers: Professionals and Students" in the Introduction.

This myth is a symptom of insecurity. Poor readers know total recall is an impossible task, and they hide behind it. It allows them to say, "I told you it was impossible. I can't do it." If this is a myth that you subscribe to, stop and evaluate your reading situation and requirements. You need to set achievable targets. Assess your familiarity with the subject, define your goals for this reading, and decide what you need to remember.

The Brain and Reading

When you pick up a book with the intention of reading all or part of it, what happens? Your eyes see the words on the pages. The words are made of letters, or symbols, which you also recognize. Each word evokes an image and a meaning: The word is understood. Next, each word is part of a sentence. You connect the words and understand their meaning. You then relate the information in one sentence to other sentences and to the rest of your knowledge: This is comprehension. Depending on how often you use this information, you retain this comprehension for a short or long period.

In summary, when you read, you perform the following tasks:

■ Visual recognition of the symbols.

■ Assimilation of the symbols into meaningful images reinforced by sounds or any of the other senses.

■ Integration into semantic—or related—comprehension.

■ Retention.

■ Preparation for recall.

Thus, reading is a complex process that involves different and distinctive steps and activities. It is difficult to pinpoint where reading takes place in the brain because, for each activity, you shuttle information between the two halves, or hemispheres, of the brain.

The brain consists of two hemispheres, the left and the right, that perform different functions. Each hemisphere specializes in certain types of activities (see Figure 1.1).

In right-handed people, the left hemisphere deals with numbers, language, and analytical thought. It processes ideas sequentially or works in a step-by-step or linear manner. The right hemisphere is better at handling concepts of wholeness, patterns, recognition, visual imagery, space, music, and rhythm, and processes ideas simultaneously or in parallel.

Many left-handed people have these brain processes reversed. Apparently over 90 percent of right-handed people, but only about 60 percent of left-handed people, deal with numbers, language, and analysis in the left hemisphere of the brain (see A. Searleman). We do not yet know why this difference exists.

The two hemispheres are connected by an intricate mass of nerve cells called the corpus callosum that works in rather the same way as a telephone: It links the two sides and makes them communicate.

At first appearance, reading is linear; it seems to be a step-by-step approach since it deals with a sequence of words. This description would make it an activity that, for the majority of peo-

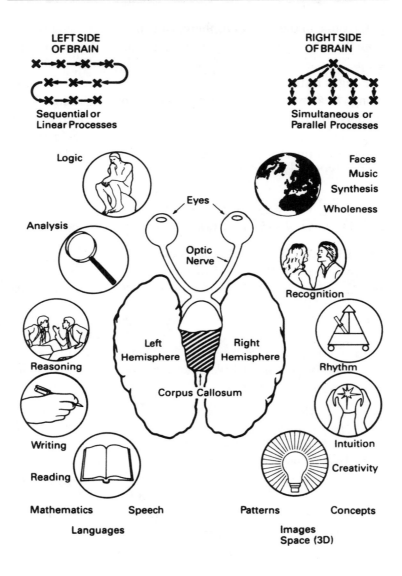

FIGURE 1.1 View from above or plan of the brain.
Activities listed for most right-handed people.

ple, is done in the left hemisphere. But efficient reading is more than that. It requires the use of visual imagery: It demands that some "whole" be seen, and that a pattern be anticipated. Also, reading is faster and easier if a rhythm is imposed as we move along. Reading involves using *both* sides of the brain. Skilled readers shuttle information automatically and unconsciously from left to right and vice-versa. Active reading forces the reader to connect ideas simultaneously and to think faster.

How Do You Read?

Let's find out. The passage that follows will assess the speed at which you read, the extent of your comprehension, and the habits that you have. Please observe the following instructions:

1. Have a stopwatch or a watch with a second hand ready.

2. Choose a comfortable place to read where you will not be interrupted.

3. Try to read as you would normally: Don't speed up or slow down because it is an exercise.

4. Have a notebook by your side.

5. Note the time when you start and when you finish reading the passage.

6. Read the passage *once only*, from "Quote" to "Unquote."

Quote.

The men who, at turning points of history, managed to make the French behave as a great nation and sometimes led them to victory, to grandeur, and to prosperity are the

immortal heroes of French history. School children recite
their names like those of saints in litanies. Among them
are (as François Maurras said) "the Forty Kings who
made France": Clovis, the king of the Franks, who gave
the country its name and its religion, Hugh Capet, the
first king, Philippe Auguste, Saint Louis, Henry IV,
Louis XIV. . . . Added to them, there are a young peas-
ant girl, Jeanne d'Arc, and one fanatical and meticulous
organizer of bureaucracy (he and his men worked sixteen
hours a day), centralizer of power, spinner of meticu-
lously intricate legal nets, promoter of all kinds of state-
owned or controlled industrial activities, founder of the
merchant navy, reformer of taxation, creator of the "ca-
dastre" (the register of all lands and their owners) and the
Bibliothèque Nationale. He gave the Académie, of which
he was a member, thirty-nine of its famous forty arm-
chairs (one rich "Académicien" had brought his own
from home). This man was the previously mentioned
Jean-Baptiste Colbert. There were two such heroes in the
last century alone, less than thirty-seven years apart, an
uncle and his nephew of the same name, Napoleon, the
former speaking French with a Corsican accent, the latter with a German accent, both raised to power by the
fear of the people in moments of turmoil and danger.
Phillipe Pétain was the penultimate. De Gaulle, of
course, was the last. At perilous times, the French look
for, to mention some examples, a victorious general in the
most recent war (Napoleon Bonaparte; Marshal Patrick
Mac-Mahon, duke of Magenta, first president of the
Third Republic; Pétain, the defender of Verdun); or a re-
storer of centralized administration and rigorous finance
(the two Napoleons, Raymond Poincaré, Valéry Giscard
d'Estaing). In war they want a resolute, unflappable,
and unstoppable leader like Georges Clémenceau or
Charles de Gaulle. No such man is always available, to be
sure, and at times public opinion pins its hopes, *faute de*

mieux, on some picturesque character such as flash-in-the-pan Pierre Poujade, a shopkeeper who stirred up masses of protesting taxpayers in the 1950s, or the poor general, Georges Boulanger (1837–1891), on his white charger, who seemed for a while in the 1880s a serious threat to the Republic but soon lost his prestige, his followers, and his nerve, and pathetically killed himself on the tomb of his recently dead mistress, Marguerite Crouzet Vicomtesse de Bonnemain, in the cemetery of Ixelles in Belgium.

These heroes of French history are proudly remembered and universally worshipped only after their deaths. When alive they all had an appalling time. Their job was always an ungrateful and dangerous one. They had to collect taxes, levy reluctant soldiers, defend themselves from dastardly plots, avoid being murdered, suppress mutinies and rebellions, and often fight bloody civil wars. Some of them were killed by assassins. Few Frenchmen really like a stern ruler, just as few people like bitter medicines. Nobody likes the impartial application of the law. Colbert died cursed by everybody, hated by Louis XIV, the king he had made great and powerful, and had to be buried secretly, at night, to avoid hostile demonstrators who might have snatched his body from the coffin and torn it to pieces. Louis Philippe was dethroned by a revolution in 1848 and fled, because his prudent despotism, his love of the *juste milieu*, common sense, and the lack of imagination had enriched France but bored the bourgeoisie. Obviously the French (like most people) love their country to be great and glorious but are reluctant to pay the price. "Il faut payer pour être la France," de Gaulle pithily warned them in vain more than once.

Unquote.   643 words

This passage is taken from *The Europeans* by Luigi Barzini. The chapter it is taken from is titled "The Quarrelsome French."

Estimating Your Reading Speed

How to Calculate Your Speed

This is the formula to apply for the preceding quotation:

$$\text{Speed} = \frac{\text{No. of words in passage (643)}}{\text{minutes}}$$

Say you took 2 minutes and 35 seconds to read this passage.

$$2 \text{ min } 35 \text{ sec} = (2 + 35/60) = 2.58 \text{ minutes}$$

$$\text{Speed} = \frac{643}{2.58} = 249 \text{ words per minute}$$

General Formula for Speed

There is another way to assess your reading speed. This other approach is used when you read material that you have chosen, and you control the test reading time you wish to devote to it.

$$\text{Speed or words per minute} =$$

$$\frac{(\text{words per line}) \times (\text{lines per page}) \times (\text{pages read})}{\text{Time}}$$

If you use this formula, you should select a reading time in advance and stop when it has elapsed. Choose one, two, five, or ten minutes for your test read. Use an alarm clock to tell you when the set number of minutes has elapsed. If you stop reading three-quarters of the way down the page, divide your page into quarters. For example, if you have read three and three-quarter pages, you have read 3.75 pages. If your passage has a lot of short lines, use your judgment to make up full lines, and estimate the fraction of a page that the words fill.

Comprehension

This book does not ask you to answer comprehension tests. Reading is an individual task. Your level of comprehension depends very much on your previous knowledge or familiarity with a subject and your ability to concentrate. You, the reader, are best able to assess this. There are some questions to ask yourself about the passage you have just read (Barzini, "The Quarrelsome French") in order to check your comprehension:

- Have I got the general idea of what this passage was about?

- Is it sufficient for my present purpose?

- Am I missing some of the details? If so, does it matter?

- Do I understand enough of what I have read, so far, to continue?

Thus, comprehension is subjective, and the quality or level of your comprehension will vary according to what you read and your purpose in reading it. A flexible approach, which includes different reading speeds, will help you adapt to different comprehension requirements.

Good comprehension encompasses:

- Being able to select and understand what you need.

- Retaining and recalling that information.

- Connecting this new information to existing knowledge.

Selecting and understanding what you need is made easier by reading with an objective in mind. It will give you the freedom to abandon unnecessary detail without feeling guilty.

The more you use this new information the greater will be your long-term retention. A method for increasing your recall is developed in the next chapter.

To connect new knowledge with old, ask yourself questions about the material you have just read and relate it to what you already knew. In this way, you modify, update, and enlarge your knowledge consciously. You can also discuss the subject with others, or summarize it in a report. These methods involve you physically in the process of comprehension and are tests in determining whether the material has been assimilated correctly.

Checklist for Recognizing Bad Habits

Determining your reading speed is only one of the factors that you are evaluating. Possibly you have other bad reading habits.

Do you agree with George Crabbe (1754–1832), who wrote:

Habit with him was all the test of truth,
It must be right: I've done it from my youth.

or with Marcel Proust (1871–1922), who wrote:

The firmness of a habit is usually in proportion to its absurdity (La constance d'une habitude est d'ordinaire en rapport avec son absurdité).

Habit is not taught but is acquired. Habit, as defined by the Oxford English Dictionary, is "a tendency to act in a certain way acquired by frequent repetition of the same act." There are two types of habits that relate to reading: good habits—habits that help and reinforce efficient reading—and bad habits—habits that hinder efficient reading. Chapters 2 and 3 aim at replacing your negative habits with positive ones. Changing habits is no easy task. Habits are engrained deeply, and have become a part of your routine.

In the passage about the French that you read did you:

■ Hear the words in your head as you read (subvocalized)?   yes   no

■ Read one word at a time?   yes   no

■ Go back and reread because you lost the meaning?   yes   no

■ Have problems remembering what it was about?   yes   no

■ Experience difficulty in maintaining your focus on the page?   yes   no

■ Find that your concentration wandered off?   yes   no

If you have more than one bad habit—the number of "yeses" in the list above—list them in order of their severity for you and go to the chapters in this book that deal specifically with them. This book, like many books, gives you a lot of advice, much of which you do not need. Therefore, read only those sections that you do need to make you a rapid reader. Practice skimming now.

CHAPTER TWO

Minimizing Bad Reading Habits—And Maximizing Positive Ones

In this chapter . . .

Improving your reading ability requires a series of step-by-step exercises designed to eliminate the negatives in your reading behavior and to accentuate the positives. In this chapter the bad habits common to many normal or poor readers are discussed.
They are

- Over-checking your reading and subvocalization.

- Not eliminating procrastination and interruptions.

■ Letting stress overwhelm you when faced with too much to read or with physical difficulties linked with reading, such as dyslexia.

You are told what the habit is, how it impairs your reading, and how it can be cured. Next, the chapter develops those positive habits you need to build on or strengthen:

■ Increasing your motivation.

■ Improving your concentration.

■ Training your memory to be better.

When this chapter has been digested, you will be ready to get down to the drill of improving your reading skills.

Reducing Subvocalization

Subvocalization is hearing the words in your head, or saying the words to yourself as you read them. All readers do this to some degree. It is a bad habit when it is frequent rather than occasional. Moving your lips when you read is the extreme form of subvocalization. If you subvocalize frequently, you need to understand why. When you learned to read, you said each word aloud to reinforce the relationship the particular order of letters conveyed as a word. Later, as you gained speed, reading aloud was discouraged.

However, some readers never lose this checking mechanism. They were not taught to modify their reading habits. They particularly were not taught to read words in a group, rather than singly. A fluent reader does not need to "hear" the words to understand the meaning.

Reducing subvocalization is easy. You must understand that you can subvocalize only a limited number of words before it slows you down. If, for example, in the speed exercise of Chapter 1, you achieved a speed of 200 words per minute and you wish to double it, you have to drop some subvocalization. You simply must force yourself to read faster. Then you won't have time to hear the words. At first you may feel a little disoriented. You will feel that you do not understand what you are reading. But persevere and trust yourself!

As you gain speed, you will find that you are converting the sounds into pictures—as images. Readers have the ability to visualize. When reading and visualization are combined, both speed and comprehension are high. The text becomes a slow-motion movie.

To practice visualization, start with simple words. When you see the word *house*, picture in your mind a house. As you get better at visualization, words describing abstracts will become shapes, colors, or pictures in the same way as concrete words. Then you will be reading using both sides of your brain as described in Chapter 1.

Reducing Procrastination and Interruptions

Slow readers tend to put off reading as much as they can for as long as they can. If you belong to this group, you need to understand the reasons for your behavior. It is because either:

1. You perceive reading as an unpleasant, long, tiresome task; *or*

2. The material is complex and overwhelming, and you do not know how and where to start.

These reasons for delay have to be overcome. If you find reading unpleasant and tiresome, you can either:

1. Tackle it cheerfully, because it cannot be avoided; *or*

2. Do it grudgingly, harming yourself in the process with negative feelings.

If the material is complex and overwhelming, you need to follow these rules:

1. Start as soon as possible. Remember the Chinese proverb: "A thousand-mile march starts with the first step."

2. Divide the material into chunks.

3. Take a five-minute rest every twenty to thirty minutes. This makes the going easier and raises your concentration level.

4. Give yourself a pat on the back. Consider what you have already achieved. Tell yourself it's not *that* complicated. (That's why breaking the material into chunks is important.)

5. Commit yourself to deadlines, and end your reading at the allotted time.

Preparing for serious reading means getting away from the telephone. It means telling others that you are going to study a document and do not want to be disturbed. It could mean shutting your door or hiding in a quiet part of the house, or having your secretary take the phone calls and discourage visitors for a while. As long as you do not isolate yourself too often and you return phone calls, people—on the whole—will respect this private time. Alternatively, you could go to the office early or stay late. Perhaps a quiet hour at home before your workday starts is the answer. Whatever is best for you, develop a regular habit to get through that material that piles up in your in-tray.

The preceding recommendations are simply common sense. But all of them are linked with efficient use of time and, thus, reinforce better reading habits.

Reducing Stress

All of us experience stress at times. But stress is subjective. What may be stressful to you may not be so to someone else. In his book *Understanding Organizations*, Charles Handy distinguishes between pressure and strain. Pressure can be beneficial and stimulating when it helps people meet deadlines or increases their performance. Strain is damaging when people live daily with anxiety, fatigue, or harassment.

Some pressure is beneficial. Through brain and glandular processes, it stimulates the production of certain hormones, such as growth hormones and adrenaline, which increase the body's metabolic rate. The production rate of some other hormones is decreased. The hormone balance of the body is thus tilted to help the body achieve the task at hand. If this imbalance is short term, no harm is done. If the situation is prolonged over many days or weeks, however, damage, such as high blood pressure or lowered resistance to disease, may occur (see Winter and Winter).

It is important that you analyze how stressful your life is. Make a list of things that cause you strain at work and at home. If you are plagued with a feeling that you are always fighting a losing battle—the "one-damned-thing-after-another" syndrome—you will not be able to concentrate and absorb written material. The strain that you experience overwhelms your motivation. It reduces your flexibility and heightens your tension.

Improving your reading may be a way for you to reduce a stressful situation. If this is the case, you may have to help the process by changing your lifestyle. This change could take the form of meditation, more physical activity, or taking breaks at regular intervals, not only during the year but also as part of your daily routine.

Alvin Toffler found that managers thriving under pressure (stimulating stress) have developed "stability zones." For some, stability is found in the family, with a spouse as an active partner. For others, it is the refuge provided by daily routines, for example, reading, exercising, or taking a nap at the same time every day.

Reduce the Effects of Dyslexia

Most poor readers have nothing intrinsically wrong. They simply find acquiring reading skills more difficult than learning, say, arithmetic or computer languages or music. However, some poor readers have an emotional or a medical reason for their learning difficulty with reading. *Dyslexia* simply means the learning difficulty caused by a medical problem. The term *learning difficulties* covers symptoms caused by emotional or linguistic problems and a variety of medical causes. *Specific developmental dyslexia* is used when the problem can be medically categorized, and it is usually diagnosed in childhood due to the obvious symptoms (see McAuslan).

Much progress has been made in the past ten years toward an understanding of what dyslexia is, but there is an enormous amount still to be learned and understood. Dyslexia can vary from a very mild form, manifest only during childhood, to a form that continues to cause substantial difficulties throughout life. Dyslexia may be a consequence of partial deafness when young, or may be induced by emotional tension or some brain malfunction. It is unlikely that anyone with a substantial degree of dyslexia would read this book.

But what of the person who has not been diagnosed as having a learning difficulty or dyslexia, but who privately has to struggle hard to keep up with his or her contemporaries? How do you identify this person?

First, there is the obvious evidence of difficulty in learning reading skills. Then there might be more specific symptoms of dyslexia, including an inability to distinguish left from right, or confusing objects with their mirror images. This is called *crossed laterality*. It is manifest, for example, by confusing *b* with *d*, or confusing the spelling of *from* and *form*. People with severe dyslexia may read *puppy* as *small dog*, or *Belgium* as *Holland* (see Anthony Smith). The characteristics common to these pairs of words indicate that the brain makes many correct associations, but fails to select the single, correct word at the end of the reading/visualizing/recall process.

Other symptoms of dyslexia, which are not at all uncommon, include:

- Ambidexterity.
- Lack of concentration.
- Clumsiness.
- Defective speech.

Readers of this book are not likely to have these symptoms to a significant extent. However, many well-known people have displayed one or more of these symptoms and have successfully overcome the handicap.

It is best for someone with a significant learning difficulty to seek professional help. But if you suspect you may have a mild form, you can help yourself to read faster by using a multisensory approach. You need to learn to read using, simultaneously, as many of your senses as possible. You acquire such a capability by drill. For example, here are a couple of very simple practices:

- The use of a guide—a finger or pointer run vertically down the center of the page at a reasonably fast speed— is one. The eyes are forced to follow the guide. This improves reading discipline and speed. (See Chapter 3 for details of "pacers" to gain reading speed.)

■ Moderately dyslexic persons sometimes have erratic eye movements. A very simple visual aid to train the eye to move horizontally may correct this problem. The aid is a window (slot) cut in the center of a large postcard. The window is the shape and size of one line of print. As the window is run down the page, the eye is limited to horizontal movements since the window shows only one line at a time.

Sensory assistance can help your reading in other ways. Link the read words (or groups of words) to as many sensory impressions as possible. Groups of words can be hooked on to images (little scenes described by the text) or your knowledge of the light, sounds, smells, or touch of objects associated with the text you are reading. A young person may be helped if the observed scene is linked to reading. In the extreme, if a brown, furry cat in the garden is crouching to catch a bird, the keywords of this scene may be written down (possibly in brown ink), and by touching the cat (probably later), and smelling the garden (maybe the grass has been cut recently). In this way connections may be established between the words and other senses.

Improving Concentration

If you reach the bottom of a page and you do not remember what you have read, your concentration is poor. You have allowed your mind to wander off; you have given in to distractions. External distractions can be greatly reduced if you minimize disruptions as was mentioned earlier. But reading and working in a noisy environment are quite possible when the mind learns to filter out the distraction. Another aid to concentration is to read at the time of day that suits you best; some people perform better in the morning, some late at night.

The environment in which you read and work is important. Although daylight is easier for your eyes, any comfortable light, if it is not too bright or too dull, is adequate. For body comfort, the temperature should be about 68 to 74 degrees Fahrenheit (20 to 24 degrees Celsius). However, most people's brains work better at about 66 degrees Fahrenheit (18 degrees Celsius). The best posture for most people is one that puts a minimum of strain on muscles. Therefore, a chair that supports your legs, particularly the thighs, comfortably and allows you to lean forward slightly is recommended.

To help you eliminate internal distractions—letting your mind wander off to more attractive thoughts—model yourself on children. Children seldom concentrate on anything for long. But when they do, they get totally immersed in the task at hand. If fifteen minutes of reading at a stretch is all that can hold your interest, then so be it. Give it your best and stop as soon as your attention lapses. But as you leave the reading, summarize, on paper or in your mind, the essential points of what you have just read.

As you discover and develop your rapid reading ability, you will find that the most powerful way of avoiding internal distraction is to anticipate what you are about to read. A big help here is to start the reading by having an overall idea of the work. Treating a book as a whole is described in Chapter 4.

Improving Memory and Recall

The ability to quickly grasp the overall contents and general idea of a document helps save time, and keeps readers from becoming sidetracked and bored. The technique of skimming a document to pick up an idea of the overall contents is described in Chapter 3.

One key factor that hinders quick comprehension of a document and detracts from long-term retention of new knowledge might be called "interference caused by subsequent learning." New learning can interfere with the recall of material learned previously. The solution to this is *chunking*. Arrange your reading and learning in time chunks of only one document or subject. Change documents or subjects only after a refresher period or after a different activity has been performed. This prevents knowledge of a new subject from interfering with a subject learned earlier.

Psychologists have long known that retention of knowledge decreases with time, particularly if the knowledge is not revised or used. The graph in Figure 2.1 illustrates how retention and recall ability decays. Researchers have demon-

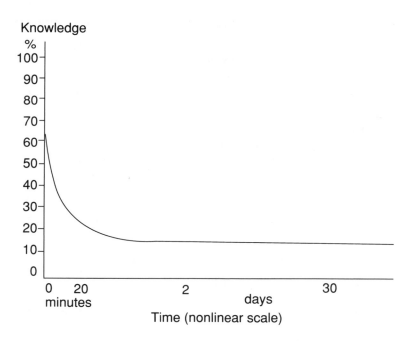

FIGURE 2.1 Knowledge recall ability versus time.
Note that 0 time is the time when 100% knowledge was acquired through sight, sound, smell, touch, or taste. *(After Hermann Ebbinghaus, about 1885.)*

strated recently that, given the correct stimulus, we can remember everything. This shows that we retain perfectly what we do every day; the problem starts when we try to retrieve or recall this information.

Why do we forget? "The easiest answer is, we don't," writes Professor J. Z. Young. We have many subconscious memories. The problem lies in the fact that we have not yet mastered a system for retrieving them. A clue to one retrieval technique is provided by a man, the workings of whose extraordinary memory have been documented (see A. R. Luria). "S," a failed journalist, could remember perfectly any nonsense list or mathematical formula or other set of data many years after it had been given to him. "S" innately used a system based on incorporating or combining new data with the data he already knew. He connected mentally, or "hooked," in his mind the new items to old familiar objects, making strong images through which he could recall the new data.

For example, when he was given a complicated formula, a part of which was perhaps like

$$h = \sqrt{981.F \times vm^2} \ldots$$

he would build a little story around it and facts in his life. Henry (h), an old friend, has given him a ruler ($=$) with which he is going to measure the bare roots ($\sqrt{}$) of a tree. The tree is 981 centimeters high, but F(reda) is cross ($\times$) and very mad (vm), in fact, doubly so (^{2}) . . . and so the story would build up, causing enormous quantities of data to be remembered and be retrievable.

Using Recall Patterns

In reading you can use a system, as described in "How to Improve Memory and Recall," for linking ideas or areas of knowledge. To keep the information fresh in your mind, use recall patterns.* The principles are simple:

- Write the main idea in the center of a page.

- Add associated ideas branching from the center.

- Use keywords that summarize a train of thought.

- Write in capitals rather than script for legibility.

Figure 2.2 is an example.

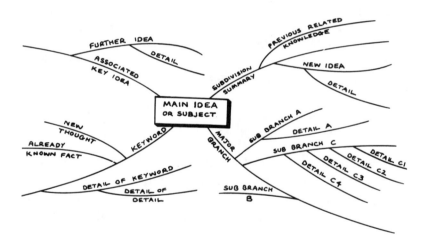

FIGURE 2.2 Example of recall pattern.

Now, apply these principles to the passage you read earlier about the French. The following example (see Figure 2.3) is

*Tony Buzan calls them "Mindmaps."

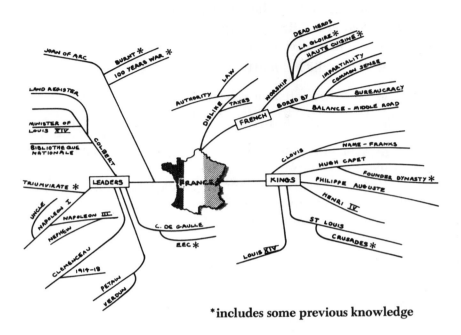

*includes some previous knowledge

FIGURE 2.3 Example recall pattern recording notes on France.

not the only way of summarizing the passage. To show how you connect old and new knowledge, the pattern has included assumed previous knowledge.

The advantage of recall patterns over linear notes is that you organize the information yourself and do not have to follow the plan expressed by the author. Thus, recall patterns allow you to hook new pieces of information to old immediately, and allow you to tailor the information to the emphasis that you, rather than the author of the book, require.

Should you have trouble, particularly at the beginning, in following your own structure, remember Kipling's poem:

I keep six honest serving-men
(They taught me all I knew);
Their names are What and Why and When
And How and Where and Who.

If you have difficulties assembling your recall pattern, What, Why, When, How, Where and Who will guide you. Apply them to each of the major subheadings of the subject you are working on.

Recall patterns have other uses, such as helping to generate ideas quickly. Cristina Stuart explains another use in connection with preparation for speeches in her book *How to Be an Effective Speaker*.

CHAPTER THREE ===

Becoming a Rapid Reader

In this chapter . . .

You select a book and prepare for exercises that teach you the technique of rapid reading. It is recommended that you complete all the exercises in about one hour. There are seven exercises in all:

■ Initial reading speed exercise.

■ Motivation.

■ Overcoming regression.

■ Using peripheral vision.

- Using a guide as a pacer.

- Conditioning.

- Consolidation.

Each exercise is introduced by a description. You practice the step once; an analysis follows. First you improve eye movements by reducing the number of fixations, then you increase comprehension speed to match the reading speed.

Throughout all exercises keep a record of your speed and comprehension. If your eyes get tired, do exercises to rest them. Finally, there is advice on how to maintain and increase the new reading speed you have reached.

Preparation for Reading

This chapter shows you the technique for becoming a rapid reader. To familiarize yourself with the material and to learn to anticipate, browse through the whole chapter, looking at the subheadings, the diagrams, and the summary at the beginning of the chapter. To work through this chapter, doing the exercises with a cooperative friend, should take about one hour.

Have a stopwatch or clock, a sheet of paper, and a pencil by you. Set up a chart, as shown in Figure 3.1, on the paper. Use this chart to record your progress.

Ensure that the lighting is sufficient. Minimize possible interruptions. Choose a comfortable chair and place it by a table. (In some of the exercises below, it is best if you have the help of a friend.)

Now, select a book. It is important that you choose a book that is interesting and light. Go for a novel, avoiding classics or humorous books. You are going into the shallow end of the pool for a few exercises before plunging into the deep end. It is

Exercise	Speed	Comprehension
1. Initial reading		
2. Motivation		
3. Overcoming regression		
4. Peripheral vision		
5. Using a guide		
6. Conditioning		
7. Consolidation		

FIGURE 3.1. Results of reading exercises.

better to tackle the technique with a document that is easy to understand than to multiply the difficulties by adding deep philosophy or strong humor.

New books, particularly paperbacks, should be broken in. A book that wants to shut all the time is not helping you to read it. Place the spine of the book on the table. Open the book at regular intervals, starting roughly at page 30. With the palm of your hand, press the book open several times along the inside spine of the book. Repeat every thirty pages or so, to the end. Do not open the book in the middle by bending the covers backwards to meet: This breaks the spine of the book, and the pages will soon fall out.

The overall objective of this chapter is to make you a better reader. That will mean building on what you already know, and perhaps changing one or two of your past habits.

Now, think positively: You *can* read faster!

Initial Speed

Set yourself a reading time—two, three, or five minutes— and set your watch. Start reading the book, as you do normally. When the time is up, make a mark with your pencil where you stopped and calculate your speed, using the formula given in Chapter 1. Record your speed on the table from Figure 3.1. Also give yourself a mark between 0 and 10 to express your comprehension. This mark must reflect what *you* think you got from the reading. Do you have a good, general idea of what you read? Did you miss some parts, or have you forgotten them already? Is it important? Can you go on? Evaluating comprehension each time you do a reading test will give you a rough idea of your reading progress. You will work on comprehension in greater detail later.

The reading speed for the average English-speaking person is between 200 and 300 words per minute. If you are slightly below, you are still within the average. If you are above, you have a head start. If you are very much below, you will have to pay attention to your faults and practice to correct them.

So, you are now equipped with an initial, or reference, reading speed that you are going to improve.

Motivation

Your objective now is to double your reading speed. Whatever you achieved in the first exercise, aim to double it. Suppose that if you double your speed, you will win a fantastic prize.

Now, take the book again, and start reading from the last pencil mark. Read for the same amount of time as you did for Exercise 1. Mark the book with the pencil where you stopped. Note your speed and comprehension at Exercise 2.

You should have achieved a higher speed than before; or, indeed, you may have doubled your speed. You have experienced motivation. Motivation is the basic step that you have to apply every time you pick up something to read.

Poor readers lack motivation because their experience of reading has not been rewarded. To overcome this problem you need to:

■ Establish objectives.

■ Read in *short* bursts.

Before you proceed with the other exercises, it will help if you set an objective. In the future, your objective will be to concentrate either on the plot or the main character. After these exercises, when using rapid reading, you will search for all the facts about chemical x and its derivatives, for example, or for everything relating to current cost accounting methods. Decide on your objective and pay scant attention to everything else. Apply this principle now, with the novel you are reading.

My objective is _____.

Overcoming Regression

Ask a friend to sit opposite you about one yard away. Hold your book up, but so that he or she can see your eye movements over the book while you read two or three lines. Ask your friend to describe your eye movements. You may also like to watch your friend's eye movements while she or he reads. Your descriptions will probably follow the diagram shown in Figure 3.2. Each balloon represents the eyes resting on a word or group of words. In the figure, the eyes go forward five times, skip backwards three spaces, then go forward four more times.

That is, the eyes move with jerky movements, or *saccades*. They take in a word, or group of words, and recognize the shape of the letters; the brain recalls the meaning of the word, or words; then the eyes go on to the next word, and then to the next. At each word the eye–brain process takes place. The eyes may go back to check what was read before—perhaps because there was a foreign name, or because a word was unfamiliar. Then the process starts again, until the eyes reach

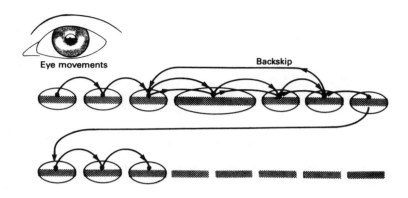

FIGURE 3.2 Eye movements.

the end of the line and then . . . zoom . . . , like a typewriter, the eyes start again on the next line.

Every time the eyes stop on a word, it is called a *fixation*. Untrained eyes will fixate six to eight times per line. Every time the eyes go back to check on a word, it is called *regression*, or backskipping.

A fixation can last from a split second to one second in very slow readers. One of the first things that you should try to do is to reduce your number of fixations to, say, four per line. And the first principle you are to put into practice is to eliminate regression. This will help you to read smoothly. The smoother your eye movements, the faster you read.

Why do you regress? Because you are unsure of what you read and think that you have missed something important. That may be true, but it is inefficient. There are two possibilities: either what you read is important and the author will mention that word again, or it is not—so why worry about it?

Imagine you are watching a movie. The action is fast-paced and confusing. Do you ask the projectionist to stop the film and rerun it? Probably not. You hope the rest of the movie will make sense. You trust the director. In the same way, trust the writer.

As you go on and you pick up speed, avoiding regression will become easier. The speed will make you concentrate more, which, in turn, will heighten your overall comprehension and will encourage you to anticipate. Regression will become unnecessary.

Now pick up your book and read for the same amount of time as you did before. Mark your book with a pencil where you stop. Calculate your speed, and record speed and comprehension at Exercise 3.

Peripheral Vision

Sit opposite a friend, about a yard apart. Have your friend hold his or her index fingers, tips touching each other, between your faces, at the distance from you where you normally hold a book. Your friend will now move his or her fingers apart, horizontally, slowly. Look at your friend's eyes, not the fingers. When one of the fingers goes out of your field of vision, tell your friend to stop moving it. Do the same on the other side. Now look at the space between the two fingers. Repeat the exercise, with the fingers moving vertically. (See Figure 3.3.)

You can determine your peripheral vision by yourself if you stare at *one* letter in a line of print. Place a finger on the letters each side of it. Then move the fingers apart until you can no longer recognize the recently uncovered letters. The distance between the fingers is probably wider than you had expected. It represents your peripheral vision. You use peripheral vision every day, when you drive, for example. Without moving your eyes, you notice that a light is changing color, a child is about to run across the road, and so on. All the while you are concentrating and looking straight ahead.

When it comes to reading, however, you make little use of

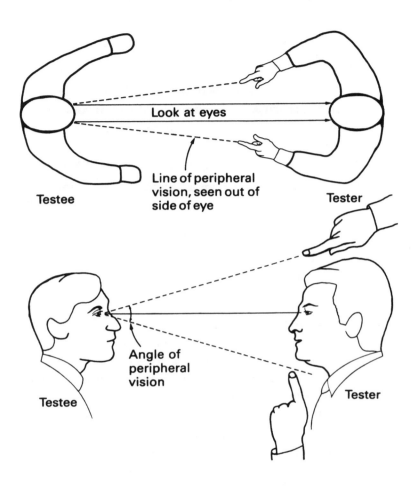

FIGURE 3.3 Top: Horizontal peripheral vision assessment.
Bottom: Vertical peripheral vision assessment.

this peripheral vision if you look at only one word at a time.
Focus your eyes on a particular word in a line of print, then
try to read the words on either side. With training, you can
take in several words at a time (in one fixation) so that you
now read as shown in Figure 3.4. Note that the eyes focus on

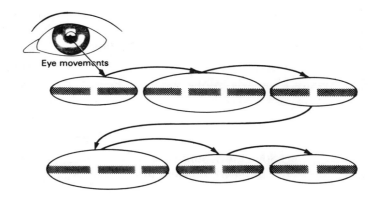

FIGURE 3.4 Eye fixations, using peripheral vision.

larger groups of letters or words than before. The eyes go to the center of each balloon and use peripheral vision to see the characters that fill the distance between the center and the edge of each balloon. Thus an inch or so at each end of a line is read by using peripheral vision, and now the eye is moving a shorter distance from left to right than it was before.

Peripheral vision is so useful it is worth exercising to improve it. Draw a vertical line down the middle of a page of text. Then, focusing only on the vertical line, at the first line of text see how many letters are seen to either side of the line. Move down the vertical line and the number of letters seen by peripheral vision will increase with practice.

a	c
xy	zo
mop	zag
acts	uvwy
and so	on and

If you don't make peripheral vision work for you, you waste a lot of effort and energy reading blank margins at both ends of each line.

Now take your book again and, at the last pencil mark, start reading, remembering to apply motivation as well as to take in groups of words in one fixation. Read for the same time as before.

When you have finished this reading exercise, mark the book with a pencil to note where you stopped, and calculate and record your speed at Exercise 4. Your speed may have gone down. Your comprehension may have gone down. There is no cause for alarm. This is a learning process, and learning is made of highs and lows. Just remember the first time you climbed onto a bicycle: You probably concentrated on watching the front wheel and kept falling off until, as if by magic, it all came together—posture, movement, looking up straight—and you were speeding down the road.

Using a Guide

Sitting opposite your friend again, ask him or her to draw a circle in the air with his or her eyes; in other words, have your friend's eyes follow the circumference of an imaginary circle around your head. Observe the eye movements and describe what you saw. Probably the eyes moved following a shape like the one in Figure 3.5.

Now, guide your friend's eyes with your finger by drawing an imaginary circle in the air. Observe your friend's eye movements again. The movement now is smoother, as in Figure 3.6.

The changes in eye movement suggest that to help your eyes move smoothly across a page, to avoid wandering off and regressing, you need to guide your eyes when you read. Initially, the guide will take your eyes along each line and down the page, line by line. This is something that you already do. If you are suffering from a toothache, you take the telephone

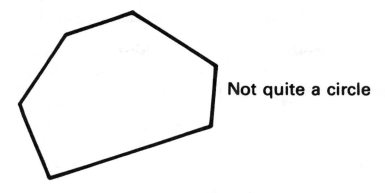

Not quite a circle

FIGURE 3.5 Unguided eye movements.

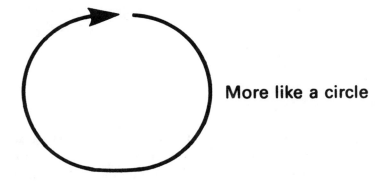

More like a circle

FIGURE 3.6 Guided eye movements.

book to look up the number of your dentist. You use your finger to search down the column for the correct name and number. Why? Because you are in pain and are trying to save time as well as not make an incorrect call. You are motivated.

So, from now on, use a finger or the tip of a pencil as a guide—whichever feels comfortable when you read (see Figure 3.7). The advantage of using your finger is that usually you have it with you, and thus you have no excuse for not using it while you read.

FIGURE 3.7 Using a finger as a reading guide or pacer.

Now put this into practice. Take your book again and start reading, for the same amount of time as before, starting at your last pencil mark. Remember to apply motivation—your objective—to avoid regression, and to group the words, fixating, say, four times or less per line.

Mark your book where you stop, calculate your speed, and record both speed and comprehension at Exercise 5.

Did your reading speed and comprehension go up? If they did, that is good. Move on to the next exercise. If you think the finger or pencil slowed you down, then move it faster in the future.

You may have found the guide a distraction, or that using it felt strange. Don't give up; persevere. You are not used to using a guide systematically, as you have just done. With practice, the guide will help you to gather speed and will focus your concentration.

Conditioning

Chapter 1 explained that reading benefits greatly from use of the right side of the brain. This includes rhythm. Some people have an innate sense of rhythm and find it easy to apply. One way to start is to move along the lines following your heartbeats, so that your finger (or pencil) traces one line per heartbeat. Do this for a page or so.

Now try to increase the pace either by saying "line, line, line" . . . to yourself, or by using a metronome set at a speed slightly faster than is comfortable. Do this for two pages, or until it feels natural.

Now you are going to practice high-speed reading with rhythm. Read from your last pencil mark, using a guide and rhythm. Start at a comfortable pace and then progressively speed up until you cannot move your guide fast enough to keep up with the rhythm. At this point you will have to use a different motion with your guide. You will have to zigzag down the page, tracing a maximum of three zigzags per page (see Figure 3.8).

To practice conditioning correctly, you need to handle your book correctly. If you are right-handed, keep your left hand at the top of the right-hand page to turn the pages, while your right hand does the zigzag movements. If you are left-handed and using your left hand as your reading guide, turn the pages with your right hand, so that the rhythm is maintained.

Set your watch for five minutes, and start from the last pencil mark. Remember that you should constantly speed up, so that you end up by moving down the pages very fast, at the rate of about one page per second. You may experience a blur during the exercise. This is normal. Your eyes need to adjust to this new way of receiving and sending information to the brain. To keep your motivation, start to look for keywords on each page. If you take in half a dozen words you are doing very well. Start now, and speed it up!

FIGURE 3.8 Fast reading conditioning with rhythm.

Do not record your speed for the first pass. It was a practice exercise. Go back to your last pencil mark, the one you made at the end of Exercise 5. Set your watch for slightly longer than before and start reading, using all the techniques you have learned so far. This time, read with comprehension in mind.

When the time is up, mark your book where you stop, calculate your speed, and record it at Exercise 6.

Your speed is probably a lot higher than for Exercise 5. Why? Because shortly before you read, you conditioned yourself to read faster. Like an athlete before a competition, you warmed up your muscles to be ready for use when you needed them. The rhythm became natural and your eyes got used to moving rapidly, following your guide. Although you read more slowly in this last exercise, you were influenced by the high-speed conditioning. People are similarly influenced by speed when they drive on the highway at a constant 55 miles per hour for a long time. When they want to take the offramp marked clearly 25 mph, they rarely slow to this: Instead, they brake a little, convinced that they are doing the required speed. The actual speed is probably more like 40 mph, and that seems very slow!

If your reading speed is considerably up, well done. Now, look into comprehension more carefully: You must bring speed and comprehension into unison. If your comprehension is adequate, skip the next few lines and go on to the next exercise.

If your comprehension is low, check a few things:

- Are you clear about your objective?

- Do you keep this in mind while you read?

- Do you move your guide smoothly underneath the lines of your page?

- Do you look for keywords along each line?

If you answer "yes" to all this, then slow down. At this stage, there is no point in having speed for speed's sake.

If your answer is "no," then pinpoint where you are going wrong and alter your habit. Then repeat the last exercise.

The speed used in the conditioning exercise is the speed you will apply when you overview a document quickly; this is described in Chapter 4. It is important that you understand the value of conditioning; practice zigzagging to enhance your concentration and speed. Once you have experienced this several times, it becomes a habit and a necessary step to recognizing quickly what you need in a document. It is only when you have mastered conditioning that you can claim to read faster and to read with flexibility: at high speed to overview, and at a more leisurely speed—a cruising speed—to read what really interests you.

Consolidation

Take your book and begin to read at the last pencil mark. Read to consolidate everything you have learned so far. You are now trying to bring speed and comprehension together. Read for at least five minutes.

When the time is up, mark your book where you stop, calculate your speed, and record it under Exercise 7.

Your reading should be more stable now. You have motivation, you have an objective, you are eliminating regression, you are grouping the words, you are using a guide to help you focus and concentrate, and you can speed up.

If you still have difficulties, which is not uncommon at this stage, repeat the exercises where you need more help. Learning a skill is unpredictable: Some wonder why they did not take it up sooner, others stumble here or there and take a little longer. Remember, you only started to read faster a few hours ago; all this is new, and you are changing some habits that have been with you for many years.

Resting Your Eyes

You may have found these exercises tiring for your eyes, or you may experience tired eyes without trying to read faster. Here are two exercises to rest your eyes.

Put your elbows on a table. Shape your hands into small cups in which you are going to rest your eyes. The word *rest* is important. Do not apply pressure to the eyeballs, as this would make the exercise useless. You should feel comfortable.

Close your eyes and create a picture. Imagine that you are

standing in a large golden-yellow wheatfield. It is a sunny summer day. Look all around you. Look to the left. There is a tall tree rising to the sky. Look at it from the trunk up; look at the green leaves against the blue sky. In the sky on the right there is a plane cruising from the right to the left. Now look at your feet—there are poppies, bright red poppies. In the distance, far away on the right, there is a church spire that rises on the horizon. Look at the whole scene again, the golden-yellow grain, the tall green tree, the blue sky and the plane moving from right to left, the poppies at your feet, and the church spire in the distance. Remember that all this should be done without feeling any pressure on your eyes.

When you take your hands away and open your eyes, things around you are much brighter and your eyes feel refreshed.

Another simple exercise is to focus on a far point—ideally out of a window. Hold the position for two or three seconds and then, without moving your head, focus on the nearest point in the room and maintain your focus for two or three seconds. Repeat the exercise five times.

Both these exercises require that you move the muscles that surround your eyes. You move them sideways and up and down. It helps to keep your eyes in good shape. Visualizing color in the dark also has a restful effect. These exercises do not take long and are particularly beneficial if you work in artificial light (see W. H. Bates).

Maintaining Your Speed

When you feel that you have mastered the techniques of reading faster while maintaining comprehension (and it may take a little longer than doing the seven exercises), how do you keep your new skill?

To keep this newly acquired skill, you need to practice about five minutes every day. I am reminded here of the famous words of a ballerina: "If you do not practice one day *you* notice it. If you don't practice for two days, the *public* notices it!" The practice consists of high-speed conditioning. The best material to practice on is a newspaper, because it has narrow columns and therefore you need only one fixation per line. Also, as a rule, a newspaper article often summarizes a situation with which you are already familiar. It is easy to be fast, until you read new information or opinion, at which point you will slow down, but still keep a fast rhythm.

You may also be wondering, how fast should I read? There is no limit. It is what *you* feel is comfortable that is the norm. Remember that flexibility is synonymous with rapid reading, and that to get at what you want quickly is as important as reading and absorbing the information.

If you wish to go faster still, start the process again, in a step-by-step manner as you have done through this chapter, focusing on speed first and comprehension later.

CHAPTER FOUR

Reading a Book

In this chapter . . .

You have learned the dynamics—the techniques—of reading faster. Now you are going to apply them, through six systematic steps. These steps are:

- Recall—what do you know already about the subject?

- Objectives—set some before you start.

- Overview—get acquainted with the whole document.

- Preview—reject the irrelevant or what you know already.

- Inview—in-depth reading of new material.

- Review—make a recall pattern of notes.

Documents have to be treated as a whole and approached as you would a jigsaw puzzle competition. This analogy is explained, together with the importance of recall pattern note taking and of adopting a flexible approach to rapid reading. Examples to illustrate the systematic approach follow in the next three chapters.

Treating a Book as a Whole

Learning is a process of pattern building. New bits of information or knowledge are significant when they fit patterns already in your mind. Your collections of patterns compose your education and experience.

When people see a pattern they do not relate to right away, they are disoriented. If they are inquisitive, they invent an explanation that fits. If they are not, or are preoccupied, they do not register the pattern. Take the picture in Figure 4.1 as an example. The dots probably have no meaning for you. However, once you know that a dalmatian dog is in the picture, you are able to find it, since you know the pattern for a dalmatian.

Books have patterns, too. The pattern is obvious in fiction, where a storyline is built around characters whom you follow through various exploits and subplots. This concept of pattern is what is meant by *wholeness*. The author had a plan, and your first task for any reading material you consider—a

FIGURE 4.1 What pattern fits this picture?

book, a report, an editorial, or newspaper article—is to discover that plan. Rapid reading of a book requires you to refer to and consider the material as a whole, to consider that book's plan.

The Jigsaw Puzzle

Imagine that you are taking part in a jigsaw puzzle competition. The prize for winning, by being the first person to complete the picture, is $20,000. You are determined to be the winner. You have been practicing solving jigsaw puzzles. Now you are in a large room with the other competitors. Each competitor is sitting at a table on which there is a sealed brown bag containing a jigsaw puzzle and its picture. At a signal, everyone starts.

What is the first thing you do? Recall your experience of solving jigsaw puzzles. Then, you tear open the bag and look at the picture. How long do you look at it? Not very long; probably a few seconds. Why? Because time is precious and because you do not need, at this early stage, to clutter your mind with details. All you want now is the general appearance, an overview of the picture. You have now fixed a target. It is a more essential step than you realize; otherwise, you start blind, unsure of the final objective.

Next, you empty the bag and arrange the pieces colored side up. As you do this, you set aside the corner and straight-edged side pieces. You are going to make the border first because it is easily recognized and has a limited number of pieces.

Next you make piles of pieces of a specific color or that have some distinctive pattern on them: a blue pile, or a pile of pieces having a black line across them, for example. Pieces that are difficult to attribute are left on the side, to come back to later.

You have already started to put the picture together, beginning with the corner pieces and straight edges. You go on to pattern blocks and color blocks. If there are strange pieces, you do not spend too long with them but put them aside with the other piles of "difficulties." You will deal with them when the picture is more complete.

The way you are working gives you the best possible chance of being among the winners. You have:

- Motivation (to win the prize, to be best).

- An objective (to complete the picture).

- Well-defined chunks of concentration (sorting all the pieces roughly, then finding the straight and corner pieces, and on to the colors).

- Postponed problems until it is easier to find a solution for them (putting aside awkward pieces for later).

The jigsaw puzzle approach should be applied to all reading material.

A Systematic Approach to Reading

You have a book to read. The following six steps are a systematic approach to reading a book.

Step One: Recall: What Do You Know?

Purpose
This is a warm-up exercise, similar to that carried out by an athlete before a competition. It also helps you identify gaps in your knowledge.

Method
Consider the title and jot down a few keywords describing what you know about the subject. This memory search puts you in a positive mode and prepares you to connect new information to the knowledge you already possess. People sometimes say that they know nothing about a subject. This is rarely true. With the wealth of information people are bombarded with through the media, travel, and conversation, is there anything so completely and utterly new that one's mind is an absolute blank? Remember what was said in Chapter 1: Reading faster is first an atti-

tude. A positive attitude starts here. As in the jigsaw puzzle competition, you get set to win the prize. You gain motivation.

Timing
This step should be done quickly, taking no more than two minutes.

Step Two: Set Objectives

Purpose
An analysis of your objectives increases your concentration and helps you to achieve them. It also boosts your confidence and helps you speed up.

Method
This most important step—establish your objectives—applies to all reading material. What are you reading it for? This seems obvious. Yet those who complain that they do not "like" reading, or that they have to read every word, or that they get bored, do so because they did not spend a few minutes establishing their personal objectives. It is the cornerstone that makes your reading more efficient and memorable.

"A man without a goal is like shooting a gun without a target," said Benjamin Franklin. The same analogy applies here. If you don't know what you are looking for, how can you find it? A book, particularly a textbook, contains a lot of information. It caters to a variety of people, and the author often does not know who those readers might be. So he or she develops some basic ideas, and links these to more sophisticated ones. It is your job to choose what you need and to concentrate on those parts, leaving the rest aside.

When you establish your objectives, trust your own existing knowledge and feel confident.

How do you set objectives? By formulating one, two, or three questions. Questions force you to look for answers and help you to keep focused. For example, when you began to read this book, the questions you asked yourself might have been:

- Will this book help me to read rapidly long office reports? *or*

- Will I be able to read fiction twice as fast? *or*

- Will I be able to stop moving my lips when reading?

Again, you must ask yourself what you want—do you want to improve your reading or information absorption ability? Is it a familiarization with the subject, a deep understanding of the ideas, or a reinforcing of your knowledge that you seek? To return to the jigsaw puzzle analogy, you now know what the picture looks like.

Be specific when you set your questions. Avoid all-embracing phrases, such as "get an awareness of," or "acquire knowledge about," which is a common mistake among poorly motivated readers. Focus each question on a clear topic.

Do not become a hoarder of useless information. What you read should be linked to your job or to a project today. Plan to use the information you acquire in the next three months. Otherwise, your job may change—or technology, or your clients—and the information will be wasted.

Timing
Don't set yourself unreasonable tasks. Allow no more than five minutes.

Step Three: Overview

Purpose
This gives you a feel of the book. You start to locate the information you seek, and you decide whether the book is worth reading.

Method
Using the high-speed conditioning learned in Chapter 3, overview the whole book. Pay attention to whatever stands out. This will include the cover, the table of contents, the index, the introduction, the summaries, the tables, diagrams, illustrations, chapter headings, and bullets (■) it contains. Flip through it very rapidly. This is not reading in the ordinary sense, but looking at the structure, presentation, and contents of the book. You are starting to sort out the jigsaw puzzle pieces.

Timing
Take five minutes for this exercise, literally flipping through the pages.

Step Four: Preview

Purpose
A preview keeps you focused. It is the art of rejection and keeps you from becoming sidetracked and distracted.

Method
Strike out, using a pencil, those parts of the document that do not help you meet your objectives. Also reject repetition, padding, or information that is already familiar. A glance, looking roughly four lines at a time, tells you whether a paragraph, a page, or even a whole section contains the information you are seeking. It is not easy to do, as most people are reluctant to actively disregard what someone has written. But is is essential if you are to keep to your objectives. When you hesitate, look again at the objectives. Be ruthless in eliminating whatever is not relevant. When your objectives are well defined, it is easy; with practice, it comes naturally. You are making piles of those jigsaw puzzle pieces that you think will be easy to do first.

Timing
Again, go as quickly as you can. The time will vary with the type of material, the way it is presented, and how well you defined your objectives. A typical time for a book might be ten minutes.

Step Five: Inview

Purpose
Inview provides you with detailed understanding.

Method
You have identified the points that interest you. You are focused and ready to read in depth. Read with comprehension in mind. Read line by line. If you have problems with comprehension, keep going: The answer may be on the next page. Continue to treat the material as a whole, building up knowledge as you read.

Your speed will depend on the nature of your book. It is important to keep a flexible approach. Use a pencil or highlighter to mark key ideas or keywords. Now is the time to apply the rhythm and cruising speed you learned in Chapter 3. Try to keep a good speed, a tempo; that is, move along comfortably, but under slight pressure.

If at the end of this in-depth reading, you have gaps in your comprehension, read the book again. It is surprising how much better your comprehension and retention are if you read the same material two or three times rapidly, rather than slogging through once, stopping at every difficulty. So, when you have a problem, make a mental note or mark the page and continue. Return to the problem later, if necessary. Inview is like assembling the edges and easy parts of the jigsaw puzzle.

Timing
Set yourself a realistic time for this task and stick to it. In Steps 1 to 4 you cut out a lot of unnecessary reading. Now you can

be generous (twenty to thirty minutes) to ensure that you achieve your objectives.

Step Six: Review

Purpose
During your review, check that all objectives are met.

Method
To consolidate what you have read, you must link it to your previous knowledge. Make a recall pattern as you did in Chapter 2. This enhances long-term memory because you hook new information onto what you already know. Making a pattern also involves early use of this new material, which means that it will become part of your knowledge. Review is also a way to check whether any fuzzy areas remain, which you may need to go back to, briefly, later.

The recall pattern is the way to summarize and link ideas. You can refer to your book, or you can do it from memory.

Timing
Depending on the amount of detail, a typical time for one book may be ten minutes, but you may need longer.

When to Make Notes

Make notes at the end of all the reading steps. This keeps you selective about the information you need to keep.

Do not make notes from the text as you read. These notes will reflect the sequence of ideas as you read them. It is inefficient because:

■ It is time-consuming.

■ The notes will be unnecessarily bulky.

- It encourages mental laziness.

- It does not indicate that you are absorbing what you read.

- The notes may not be necessary.

Notes made after the different readings contain what the document means for you. It is now part of your mental property or knowledge. To ensure long-term retention of it, you need to link it to what was already in your memory. In order to do this, you will probably use a different layout or sequence from that used in the book because the information is now yours and fits into your own experience.

Also, writing and reading are two different activities, requiring different mental and physical actions. When they are mixed, each one interrupts the other as you go back and forth between them. When they are separated, they reinforce each other.

Flexibility in Reading

"There is no one right way," wrote Peter Drucker. What is true in management in general is true for the acquisition of a skill like rapid reading. Although you have been through a systematic approach to the reading of books, there are differences between individuals and between the documents they handle. Some steps can be omitted. The next chapter looks at several specialized reports and puts this assertion to the test.

Rapid reading is like learning to cook. First you get the rules straight. You must acquire some basic principles, such as how to cook green vegetables or red meat; then you refine this knowledge with the elements for simple sauces. Once you have got the basics, and understand why things are done this way, you can adapt any recipe to your own taste. So, you must follow the rules until they become second nature. When that stage is reached, you can skip a stage, or combine two, just as you would with your favorite dishes.

Summary

These six steps are the systematic approach to rapid reading. Make sure you know and understand them. They are the tools needed to apply the dynamics—the personal reading technique or skill—learned in Chapter 3:

- Recall your previous knowledge of the subject.

- Establish your objectives: Select up to three.

- Overview: Pick up the document and get acquainted with it.

- Preview: Reject irrelevant and familiar material.

- Inview: Read carefully any new information.

- Review: Make recall pattern notes to link new and old knowledge.

Above all—*be flexible.*

CHAPTER FIVE

Applying Rapid Reading to Business Reports

In this chapter . . .

Reprinted below is a report on project procedures. You will read it according to the method described in the preceding chapters, proceeding through the six systematic steps that have been explained.

At the end of this report, you will find each step examined, with an explanation of how one person may apply rapid reading to it. Obviously these notes are only one way of tackling the report. There are many different correct answers that could emerge as a result of other people, with different viewpoints and knowledge, reading it for different purposes. Remember to be flexible!

Management Tools— Project Planning Procedures
by A. K. Redway

Introduction

This article describes procedures for managers to use to undertake a project and how to control the necessary activity once it is initiated. In order for the manager to ensure the smooth running of all activities through to a successful conclusion, he or she must use the available human resources to the best effect, commit the financial resources available economically, and meet the necessary time deadlines. This requires a significant effort in planning. The better prepared the manager and his or her staff are, the greater are the chances of the project reaching a profitable conclusion.

The following sections of this article deal with the typical elements required to make a plan, and with those factors which have to be considered and controlled in order that future activities take a predetermined course leading in the desired direction. Each one of these elements should be written up as one or more procedures to define the project for all management and staff concerned, so that all understand the background to the project, its objectives, and their responsibilities to it.

The Plan

All other factors being equal, the person or company that succeeds makes fewer mistakes than the competition. The process of doing more things correctly can be planned. It is difficult to make provision for unforeseeable factors, but contingency items can be inserted into a plan as a precaution against unexpected changes in direction.

In planning a strategy, very broadly, all normal commercial business activities may be divided into routine daily activities (repetitive paper processing or production of goods, for example) or one-time unusual exercises (a company takeover or the construction by a company of new office buildings or factories for itself). Whichever type of activity a company engages in, it requires the tools to do the job—the planning, objectives, organization, schedule, reporting procedures, and controls to monitor achievement, progress, and financing.

Among the best of tools to organize or plan purposeful activities are procedures which may be written and published to apprise all staff of the plan.

The Procedures

During the initial weeks of scoping out a scheme or project, among the many items requiring definition are the management methods by which the objective will be realized. These are the administrative or organization guidelines to be followed, as distinct from legal, political, or technical requirements. The management plan envelops and coordinates all other requirements so that, at the appropriate times, all parties who have a necessary input to the total process make their contribution toward the end product.

In general terms the main subjects dealt with in a project scope and procedures manual should be, typically:

- Project purpose or objectives;

- Job scope or size;

- Basis of feasibility;

- Division of responsibilities;

- Responsible personnel;

- Organization chart and job descriptions;

- Financing arrangements;

- Agreements—contracts;

- Schedule—program;

- Administrative arrangements and plan of execution;

- Cost and progress reports and controls;

- Legal planning and insurance; and

- Implementation or construction.

During the initial conceptual phases of a scheme, the above headings may represent proposed ideas, future developments, or plans. Then, during the progression from propositions to actual confirmed plans, the manual will evolve into a firm working document, with actual facts recorded under the appropriate headings, which will have been modified to fit in with the firmed-up arrangements or job progress.

Most of the subjects listed above require a written procedure or instruction describing what has to be done. These procedures should be specified in such a manner that all staff on the job work together in a consistent, coordinated manner. New personnel coming on to the job can soon find out how to do their duties, without disruption to the surrounding organization.

The Project Objectives
First of all a definition of the end product or objective is required, whether it is the production of a banking service or a new petrochemical plant. Undoubtedly, during the attain-

ment of the objective, changes will occur in both the end product and the method of reaching it. Flexibility is an essential ingredient of planning, execution, and achievement, but only necessary cost-effective modifications should be introduced. Also simplicity is a wholly desirable quality of all procedures and objectives; it is only too easy to swamp essentials in masses of peripheral data or methods which detract from the most effective manner of execution.

Between the conception of the idea and its realization there lies, among many other activities, the creation of a concise, simple, and clear set of procedures for the accomplishment of all essential activities. (Any other activities should be carefully reviewed for relevance and stopped immediately if not positively productive. If relevant, they should be incorporated into the procedure.)

The first activity, defining the scope of the work, may serve several functions. It may be used as the basis for economic and technical studies and for the evaluation of customer, staff, and other sociological reactions. It can be used to initiate financing activity or to stimulate interest in the planned development from political or local community groups, and, most important, to interest the ultimate consumer or customer-representative bodies.

The project purpose or objectives section of the project scope manual is a concise description of what is to be created and for what purpose. It may also mention briefly the personnel involved, the time frame, the cost, location, size of facility, etc. It must be kept concise for people to understand the whole scope of the project quickly. Subsequent sections of the manual go into detail. The first of these is the job scope.

The Job Scope

The job scope or size is not only the numerical description of the magnitude of the job. It differs from the project objectives in that it includes a list of all activities that have to be performed, such as planning, financing, construction, etc., for the completion of the objectives. It may list tasks which will be performed by other organizations. Besides describing the job scope required in order to reach the objective, it should describe briefly the objective—the end product—itself. This assists in evaluating the size of the task to be performed.

The Basis of Feasibility

Without proving the basis of the project's feasibility, time is wasted. It has to be shown on paper that the objectives are politically, socially, and physically possible. Can land be acquired? Is there a real need for the project? Will trade unions accept it? The potential financing for the project has to be described, with the economic justification for it. What will be the return on the investment? Will the product be required by the market?

Division of Responsibilities

The division of responsibilities defines the split of work between the client and the contractor. In a more detailed form, it lists the scope of the work and activities against the individual department or organization responsible for carrying them out. It is a precursor to job descriptions, and is essential, acting as a checklist so that all participating personnel know their duties and all major task requirements are undertaken.

The Responsible Personnel

The organization structure, job descriptions, and responsible personnel are closely related sections which may be described together. Personnel have to be nominated to carry out various phases and activities of the job. Working relationships have to be defined by the organization structure, and the personnel assigned to specific functions have to know what their jobs and responsibilities are by means of their job descriptions. Job descriptions are closely related to the scope and nature of the project; all activities to be performed must be allocated within the organization—even those that will ultimately be subcontracted to outside organizations—all of which will require administration from the project's central organization.

Organization Chart and Job Descriptions

In order to make clear who does what, and to whom, an organization chart is an indispensable aid. This will show in a tree or pyramid diagram the branches and relationships between the head of the organization and subsequent layers of managers and administrators down to the clerical or manual levels.

It is most important that lines of responsibility are clear—who reports to whom, who is responsible for what. Bearing in mind the very rough guideline that one leader can effectively control the work of a limited number of staff, the organization splits downwards at each level into teams of five to ten staff. Each team should foster a cooperative spirit, not only internally within the team, but coordinating with surrounding teams. This should apply whether the work is organized in matrix management or in-line departmentally.

In a matrix organization everyone has a supervisor responsible for the job or project of the moment. The staff member and supervisor need not be members of the same department, skill, profession, or trade, but they have been assigned by their departments to work together on the current job, usually in a task force formed specially for the project. They are usually full time on one project only. This is the best organizational method to use to pursue a special project.

Departmental in-line organization does not usually involve a task force, and projects are processed through each department possibly with no single person taking a special interest in any particular project. In departmental organization priority projects may founder.

The in-line structure is simpler but less flexible in meeting varying workload patterns and priorities. It is more suitable for the smaller organization—each person has only one supervisor, who is responsible for both work quality and quantity. Any staff member may work simultaneously on two or more jobs, with perhaps better time availability utilization but inferior priorities and lines of communication, as other people working on the same job may be physically located elsewhere.

Job descriptions serve several purposes. The principal benefits derived from formalized descriptions are that the duties of staff positions are made clear and thus the organization is strengthened. The description should include the position, title, supervisor and subordinates, a list of duties, experience, and educational requirements of the position incumbent. Recruitment for the position is tremendously improved. To the description can be tied accounts and personnel activities, such as salary scale.

Financing Arrangements

The present-day complexity of financing arrangements renders it advantageous for key members of most job organizations to be aware of them. The terms and conditions under which a project proceeds can have an enormous influence on the job objectives and how they are attained. Many agencies from the World Bank to local businesses want to attach conditions to money supply which will direct the ways in which certain activities are carried out. It is best if all these conditions are clarified early on in the job so that the money supply is not prejudiced. Typical restraints can include activities having to be carried out in a certain place, by a specified time, with certain staff, with goods being supplied by nominated vendors, etc. To add to the complexity of the situation, legislation may prohibit a condition, particularly when jobs cross international boundaries.

In certain circles the awareness of the realities of economics are becoming increasingly rare. However, ultimately they come home to roost. Therefore, it is imperative that the profitability of a venture is recognized and pursued, and any deviations from the plan are recognized and corrected. To this end certain aspects of the financing arrangements should be made known so that the project is set up with real economics within the objectives. This will mean that key activities are tailored to fit into the economic requirements of the objectives, and that the job will be successful.

Agreements

No present-day project of any size can proceed without a multitude of permissions and agreements. It is advisable to present an extract of agreements with other parties which affect basic items in the execution of the project. Thus, it can be assured that important aspects of agreements are produced properly into the necessary activities of the job. Factors can affect legal, labor, financial, economic, territorial, and technical aspects of the job.

Client and partners have a deep commitment to the job. Ensure that their interests are properly protected as good business ethics and the contract or agreement require.

License and royalty agreements are common in business today. Many projects are totally dependent on them. They should be entered into very carefully, and it should be made clear, in the project procedures, what they are so that they are dealt with in the correct manner. Frequently such agreements impose restraints on the licensee, which must be met if they are party to a contract.

Subcontracts, in which services are procured from outside parties, are an essential component of all projects. Procedures for acquiring and administering subcontracts should be carefully formulated and followed. If, in the course of the project, one's own company is providing services to an outside party, the scope of services should be carefully monitored to ensure conformance with the contract.

The Schedule

Time is money, and it therefore pays to plan in advance a realistic program for the development of the project's organization and its realization. A little foresight will eliminate the majority of foreseeable problems.

There are many different activities to be planned and many different ways in which the schedule can be generated. The first or master schedule is that for the overall job, from the present through to the full operation of the facility or service. This will cover the mobilization of the required organization, the preparation of the job documentation, the acquisition of equipment or services, and the actual setting-up or building of the facility or service.

The master schedule may be presented as a time-scale bar chart or a very simplified activity-node network, or combinations or variations of these. Undoubtedly, the best to use is the one most suitable or comprehensible to the users. (An excellent "management presentation" schedule is the time-scale bar chart, milestone or flag type. Here the termination of each discrete phase or activity is highlighted with a little flag. Planned and actual progress can easily be compared.)

Schedules may be drawn simply by hand, or better still put on a computer. Highly complicated networks with hundreds of activities and restraints can be quickly revised and updated periodically or whenever new knowledge is gained about the time span of an important activity.

In order to check a simple master schedule, it is necessary to break it down into phases, for example, mobilization, documentation, acquisition, and construction. Then each of these is broken down further, obtaining advice from the specialists in these areas, into tens, hundreds, or even thousands of activities which are given time durations and start restraints by preceding activities. The degree of breakdown, which should be minimized, depends on many obvious factors. Only important factors should be considered.

Planning many aspects of the job springs from the schedule. Some of the principal items are:

- Personnel requirements;

- Budget allocations/cash flow;

- Latest dates for decisions or activities;

- Job progress requirements; and

- Job controls/reports requirements.

The schedule and cost budget should be developed for maximum economy, while maintaining the ultimate objective of the job fully. The job scope, schedule, and budgets stand by as the references against which actual progress may be measured and from which any necessary modifications or corrections may be planned.

Administrative Arrangements and the Plan of Execution

Plan of execution is a term often used to describe the activities to be performed—how, when, and by whom they will be performed—in a project being carried forward from the first to final activities in the overall job schedule. The administrative arrangements will have to be made around the plan of execution. They will define the details.

Probably, the key to the execution plan is the type of organization set up to execute the job. It may be organized departmentally or by a special task force. The departmental organization is effective if the job is not large, if all the different departments are properly staffed for their work loads, and staff work best by staying in the same physical location continuously. However, a matrix staffed task force is indisputably better for a project with strict time and budget restraints set on it.

After choosing the type of organization, it is necessary to decide how a large job will be staffed and activity initiated. During the course of the job, the organization will change. It will progress through departmental contributions, grow into a full-scale task force, and then shrink at the end, unable to support enough personnel for a task force, back to a low level of departmental input.

A plan of execution concentrates consideration of the method of accomplishing a job. The head of the organization to carry out the job must be appointed, and he or she has to assemble and coordinate, in one form or another, the team or personnel to assist with the job. All these people (or the senior responsible people in each department) need to be named, and their relationships and duties in the team have to be defined by an organization chart and job descriptions or functions.

The services to be provided, when, where, how, and by whom, all need stating. A description of the sequence of events as the milestones of an objective schedule (or program) are passed helps to clarify the future requirements and planning.

Writing a job scope and procedure, containing detailed administrative procedures, follows naturally from the plan of execution, giving the detail, while the plan is written in broad terms only. The basis of all aspects of the future work must be defined, together with the objectives, estimates, schedules, meetings, and products.

Under administration it is possible to list many activities which have to be performed, such as control of communications, decisions, cash flow, design, procurement, dealing with outside entities, travel, etc. Such a list will ensure that each department or function is aware of the requirement, and fulfills it. If the activities are complex or repetitive, it is best if the methods of performing the required work are described carefully so that as the work is completed it may be checked (and corrected) against a standard.

Cost and Progress Reports
and Control

A report describes past history from which we should learn. Control is the feedback of deviation followed by corrective action.

Carrying out any job economically, on schedule and within budget, requires adequate but not excessive reports for management at all appropriate levels of the organization structure. All members or teams of an organization need to know what their work objectives are and whether they are reaching them. Thus produced work has to be measured against scheduled work, against the time schedule, and against the cost or worker-hour budget. The comparison of actual and planned figures shows deviation which is then used in corrective action feedback.

Reports can be made in many forms. The best are simple and concise. The currently reported figures, whether on schedule or not, should be reviewed. Is the schedule too long or too short? Are human resources throttling the rate of progress, or is the job overstaffed? However well or badly the job is progressing, the schedule—on which most controls are based—can be updated continuously and quality improved. By correcting for historical accuracy, the accuracy of future forecasts can be improved.

The majority of controls must, at any point in the time duration of the job, be converted into rates—or the total quantity charged to date—to be meaningful. Thus one of the best presentations of controls on generalized items or parameters, such as those listed below, is in the form of planned and actual curves plotted against time:

- Cash flow, budget committed;

- People, staff on the job, worker-hours expended;

- Products produced, drawings, documents, items of whatever the product is; and

- Consumption of raw materials, feedstock (which can include cash and time).

Any of these items may also be presented in a numerical tabular form.

Naturally, it is most important to choose the minimum numbers of the most important parameters to monitor, or control, the job. The analysis of each parameter costs a lot of time, and therefore the minimum number for proper control should be monitored. Also it is essential to analyze only those that are relevant or show what needs to be known in the simplest or quickest manner. Irrelevant statistics are a menace.

Further useful analysis can be made by checking the ratio of production numbers against the consumption of raw materials. This gives a "materials efficiency" number, for instance, so many worker-hours or dollars to make each product. Comparisons of these ratios can be highly informative (or misleading if misunderstood).

Legal, Planning, and Insurance Requirements

The legal requirements of the country in which various activities of the project are undertaken must be met. While it is not normal to list the laws of a host country, it is possible that important or unusual requirements with respect to a particular job should be highlighted. These legal requirements may cover any subject, such as international trade, boycotts, working hours, expatriate staff permits, exchange control regulations and taxes, etc. Constant vigilance has to be maintained in order not to commit breaches of the law.

The restraints that may be imposed on a project by the planning authorities may be onerous. These conditions may change the initial conception of a project considerably. It is essential that the correct specialist staff, similar in function to those in the legal field, guide the initial stages of the job through the planning complexities. Then the appropriate warning notices must be issued in the job procedure.

Insurance obligations may be similar to legal and planning requirements. As far as jobs are concerned, it is important that staff be warned of difficult areas and know how to deal with them.

Consultants

There are areas of business or expertise that are best undertaken by a specialist firm acting as a consultant. Activities in the legal, marketing, special sciences or engineering, research, economics, banking, and many other fields may fall into those areas where it is best to hire someone else to provide expertise. Naturally if one is going to use consultants in one field frequently, it may become economical to set up a department for that specialty in one's own firm.

The engagement of consultants must be undertaken very carefully, as must the writing of their contract, so that they provide only services which are really required, and so that the services and all results and backup data including, perhaps, calculations, may be terminated, or obtained at an intermediate point in the exercise, if the exercise has to be stopped before the end.

Consultants may be hired to perform a specific task, or to provide a service as requested on an intermittent basis. When first hiring consultants the full scope of work for them may be unknown (the consultant may be largely responsible for determining it). Take care that a runaway situation does not develop; carefully monitor the expenses, products, and schedules of the consultant. Similarly, the professional consultant will check that the client is asking for the right products, using them properly, and not wasting time and money.

Construction Aspects

So far the project procedures have described how the project is going to be organized. At the end of the project a new service, organization, factory or facility is going to emerge. This facility itself has to be organized (see Facilities Operation) but before that it has to be constructed. Construction may be defined as assembling various components to create a whole product. The activity of construction then requires definition and guidance. All sections of the procedure contribute toward construction, but more precise instructions are required for the assembly.

At this stage, before the project has developed far, it may be possible only to indicate the proposed or preferred method of assembly of components. Various services, contracts, or items, many of which are not firm or finalized, require future development. It is only after the shape, scope, timing, and quantity are definite that final construction can be detailed, but it is necessary at the beginning of the project to express a clear idea of the shape of the components so that during development all personnel are working on similar lines toward final interlocking assembly.

Many projects go through a phase in which there is a massive physical erection activity of mechanical components of a factory or facility. For this, decisions have to be made early in the job about how this phase will be managed, what sort of labor will be used, what the scope of subcontracts will be, what the schedule will be for getting equipment to site and placing it in position or storing it, and how progress will be monitored for schedule, budget, quality, and construction safety.

The Facilities Operation
This subject represents the ultimate estimate of the future, and, like any document describing future work (especially project procedures), will need revision whenever developments show that the way ahead is

different from that which was estimated originally. The operation of facilities covers many facets of the actual running, renewal, maintenance, and modification, training of personnel, records and parts keeping, and the planning of future development, budgets, and profitability.

After planning the services or equipment for the project, the documents covering the facility operation must be prepared. During the planning and specification stages of the project, the operability of the facility is always a major factor to be considered. Detailed consideration of the facility operation may cause modifications to be made to the original planning, but these must be minimized.

During the initial planning stage of the project, it may be necessary to mount a major study or investigation of financing, marketing, or other activities that will be continuous throughout the future life of the operating facility. Obviously it is pointless to execute a major project setting up a facility if one of the key normal activities of the facility is uneconomical. While the construction project will have been set up only after pilot economic studies, these may well be carried further as part of the design or specification stage. Presumably the secondary studies will confirm the initial results, but they may also yield important data to be built into the operating procedures.

Operating procedures, written for the normal day-to-day business of the facility, may contain subjects such as those already mentioned in this article. The minimum operating procedures for all companies are the government's requirements which call for nominated personnel in certain functions and the annual audit and accounts. The opposite extreme are the directives, instructions, and laws which control the operations of large international corporations and governments. Be-

tween these two extremes every significant facility requires its own specific operating procedures covering
items not already included in the parent organization's
procedures for management, finance, technical, and
personnel departments.

Six Steps to Reading the Report

Step One: Recall: What Do You Know About Project Procedures?

Imagine that you are in charge of building a pyramid. How
would you go about assembling the procedures that would be
required? What do you know about procedures?

- Procedures are needed to make all project staff work in the same manner and direction.

- Procedures will inform all need-to-know personnel of the project details.

- Procedures require a team, communications, team leader, computer planning, monthly reviews, dead-lines, delegation, and rules.

Step Two: Objectives: Why Are You Reading This Report?

You want to know:

- Who writes procedures and how?

- How are the procedures used by the project team?

■ Will you be able to organize other projects' activities in a manner comparable with these procedures?

Step Three: Carry Out an Overview

Do not write anything for this step. Glance through the whole report quickly, noting keywords or highlights.

The title is "Management Tools—Project Planning Procedures." That looks as if it will satisfy some of your objectives. The introduction confirms this.

Keywords—paragraph titles are:

■ Plan

■ Procedures

■ Objectives

■ Job scope

■ Feasibility

■ Responsibilities

■ Personnel

■ Organization

■ Finance

■ Schedule

■ Plan of execution

■ Cost and control

■ Legal and insurance

■ Consultants

■ Construction

■ Operation

Some of these look interesting and should be followed up in Step 5.

Step Four: Preview

Reject those parts of the article that do not add to your knowledge or do not meet your objectives. Zigzag through the report to do this. Therefore, you might cross out the following paragraphs:

- The Plan
- The Basis of Feasibility
- Division of Responsibilities
- Financing Arrangements
- Agreements
- Legal, Planning, and Insurance Requirements
- Consultants

Step Five: Inview

Read those paragraphs that remain after the rejections made in the Preview step. As you read paragraphs or sections during the Inview stage, you may find that more of these can be rejected, thus completing the Preview process and shortening the Inview stage. Other paragraphs that should be studied more carefully when reading for the second or third time can be made to stand out by underlining, or with a line in the margin, or by using a colored highlighter pen. The pace is steady and rhythmic. It is comfortable, taking several words in one fixation. It is your cruising speed.

Step Six: Review

What parts of the article supply answers to the objective requirements? You now have to make notes or a recall pattern.

You may decide to answer each objective one at a time. For objective number one, you might answer with traditional linear notes.

Who writes procedures and how?

There is no clear answer to this objective, so further reading elsewhere will be necessary. However, the first paragraph of the introduction to the report indicates that the Project Manager is responsible for getting the procedures written. The Responsible Personnel and Organization Chart sections deal with the fact that writing the procedures can be assigned to a suitable person on the team. The fourth to seventh paragraphs of Administrative Arrangements and the Plan of Execution help some way toward the objective.

How Are the Procedures Used by the Project Team?

To answer this objective, look at Figure 5.1, which shows a recall pattern:

Will you be able to organize other projects' activities in a manner comparable with these procedures?

Yes! The report lists many of the factors that have to be considered in organizing a project, and gives some guidelines for how they should be handled. Therefore it should be possible to assemble a list of factors for a specific project that will require procedures, and then to start drafting the procedures' contents.

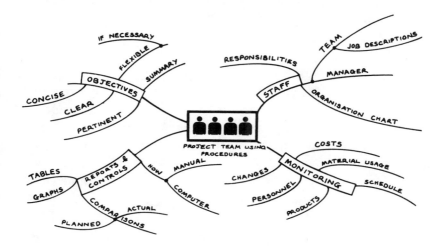

FIGURE 5.1 Recall pattern notes on project procedures.

CHAPTER SIX

Applying Rapid Reading to Legal Reports

In this chapter . . .

The systematic six-step method can be applied to material that is reputed to be precise and where every word counts. The following example is taken from *The Law Society's Gazette*.

You will go through the same steps as with the previous example report, but with different objectives in mind. Only one way is given to read the report, but there are many possible ways. The results depend primarily on the objectives you set at the beginning and what information the document contains.

The example takes the position of a layperson who wishes to expand her or his knowledge of the subject.

Time-Sharing—
The Club/Trustee System
by James Edmonds *

This is the third in a series of five articles on the subject of time-sharing. The most common structure for a time-sharing scheme is known as the club/trustee system and this article comments on that structure.

The most usual system utilized to set up a time-share scheme in the United Kingdom, Spain, Malta, or Greece is the club/trustee system. The system is also used in Portugal and increasingly in other jurisdictions.

Under the club/trustee system the promoter becomes founder member of a club. The promoter then transfers the villas or apartments to be time-shared to a trustee, to be held upon trust for the club members. The club rules divide the occupancy of each apartment or villa into 50 or 51 weekly periods, and provide that memberships are related to available occupancy periods, so that each member must be entitled to use one or more occupancy periods. The possible club membership is thus limited by the number of villas or apartments in trust and the number of weekly periods acquired by each member. The sole right of original appointment of new members is vested in the promoter, as founder member, but any member who derives title from the founder member can

*Attorney

appoint a new member in his or her place, i.e., can sell or transfer the time-share.

The reason for the spread of the club/trustee system to civil law countries, unfamiliar with the Anglo-Saxon concept of trusts, is partly due to the United Kingdom market being the largest market for time-sharing, and partly due to the unique advantages of the concept over any alternative. The system is examined in more detail in the author's book *International Timesharing* (2nd edition).

Documentation

The initial documentation required to establish a club/trustee is the Club Constitution. The club is an unincorporated association whose members agree to be bound by a common set of rules and who together elect a committee to represent their interests. The rules of a time-share club must define the powers of the founder member (to appoint the original members) and restrict those powers so as to protect the interests of the membership generally. The rules must provide for the election of a committee, and its powers once elected, the allocation of running costs between members, and many other matters of detail.

Second, a management agreement is needed. Usually the promoter is responsible for management at the outset, and incorporates a management company for this purpose. The management company is usually also made a founder member of the club, with powers for control of management to pass to an elected committee of members, once sufficient members have been appointed. The management agreement will define in more detail the allocation of expenses between members. The agreement will have to provide for different-sized units and the introduction of more units into the scheme over a period. The agreement has to set out the responsibilities of the management company in some detail.

Third, there is the trust deed which defines the responsibilities of the trustee to safeguard trust assets on behalf of club members, and to see that those assets are properly transferred, free of encumbrances, and that ongoing responsibilities (e.g., payment of taxes, insurances, etc.) are discharged, so that the assets once transferred are not expropriated or destroyed without compensation. The role and responsibilities of the trustee go far beyond this, however, and will be examined below.

The final essential is the sales contract. This must identify the parties (surprisingly some do not!), the unit, and the time periods. It should provide for payments to be made to an escrow agent (usually the trustee), not the promoter. The escrow provisions should effectively prevent the sale proceeds from being handed over to the promoter until the units have been vested in trust, free from encumbrances.

Consumer Protection

The two great advantages of the club/trustee system are consumer protection and flexibility. The keystone of the club/trustee system is of course the trustee. Provided that the trustee is independent, adequately capitalized and insured, and administratively equipped to deal with the time-share trust, a considerable degree of consumer protection can be achieved.

First, the promoter parts with his or her interest in the villas or apartments in exchange for the right to sell club memberships. Consequently, if the promoter becomes bankrupt or insolvent, a liquidator or receiver acquires only this right, not the ownership of the apartments or villas themselves. The existing members are therefore secure, and the property which they have a right to occupy will not be taken away from them.

Second, the trustee keeps, or should keep, details of every member and every unit in trust and every unit to be transferred into trust, so as to ensure that the membership is not sold more than once in the same week, and that the promoter does not obtain funds from sales in units not in trust. This is the fundamental reason why the deposit and purchase price should be paid to the trustee, and not to the promoter.

In several cases, the scheme has been set up properly at the outset, but the promoter is selling time-shares not only in units which have been bought and paid for, and transferred into trust, but also in units which have not been purchased or completed, or which are mortgaged. In the latter cases, the sale proceeds should be held by the trustee and not disbursed to the promoter until the units have been transferred into trust, free from encumbrances.

What sometimes happens is that the promoter runs into what have been called cash-flow problems. The promoter then proceeds to open an account in his or her own name, reprints the contract to provide for payments directly to him or her, and banks and utilizes the funds without telling the trustee. In the meantime the sales literature still includes references to the trustee so that purchasers are misled, believing that they are safeguarded, when that is not in fact the case. In the absence of legislation this puts the trustee in a very awkward position. Resignation by the trustee will only prejudice the interests of owners who are protected under the trust, since the owners who are protected may find it very difficult to persuade a reputable trustee to take on board what is bound then to be a messy situation.

Therefore, in a club/trustee situation it is essential either to have the money paid to the trustee, or to obtain a certificate from the trustee that the particular unit being time-shared and week being sold is covered by the trust. A trustee which does not itself maintain ownership records may not always be able to establish with certainty who are the beneficiaries, i.e., who is protected by the trust.

Third, the trustee should be responsible for administering the consumer protection aspects of the scheme, to see that moneys which are received by it are not disbursed until clear, unencumbered title to the unit in question is transferred into trust, or that it is in possession of adequate guarantees that this will happen.

Where units are being constructed, and time-shares being sold in those units, the promoter often needs funds to pay for construction and marketing expenses. In such circumstances the trustee may be prepared to release from escrow funds covered by an independent guarantee from a bank, or from a substantial corporation, or secured on other assets. In some cases the building land can be transferred to the trustee at the outset, and the trustee can release up to a percentage of the value of the asset so transferred, on the basis that if the building works are not completed, the trustee may sell the assets and use the proceeds to reimburse the time-share purchasers.

Fourth, there is the ongoing responsibility of the trustee to safeguard trust assets. In many jurisdictions the properties themselves are subject to expropriation if taxes are not paid. So the trustee must ensure that the taxes are paid on time. A similar situation can arise in relation to community charges, e.g., *communidades* in Spain. The trustee must see to it that the properties are insured against fire and other perils. When the time-share owners resell, the trustee must record the change of beneficiary. Often where time-shares are pledged as security for a loan, the trustee will hold the certificate until the loan is paid off. Again, on resale, the trustee should be in a position to advise whether the maintenance charge has been paid, or whether the membership certificate has been forfeited for nonpayment.

Finally, the independence, substance, and administrative capability of the trustee is of paramount importance. Unfortunately some promoters are unable or unwilling to persuade a reputable trustee to act. This may be because of the record of the individual behind the scheme, or because the promoter cannot afford to have funds blocked in escrow, or because the promoter is unwilling to incur the cost, or for a variety of other reasons. Also, many reputable trustees will not take on a trusteeship unless they are satisfied with the substance and qualification of the promoter. This has led to the formation by promoters of one-off trustee companies, often owned or controlled by the promoter and set up specially for the purpose. "Off-the-shelf" trust companies can be formed in many jurisdictions without capitalization requirement beyond $4. The level of capitalization of any trust company should be considered in the context of its professional indemnity policy (if any). Equally obviously, a trust company controlled, directly or through nominees, by the scheme promoter is hardly a proper guardian of the rights of those who purchase from that promoter. Again, some off-shore accountants or company formation agents are prepared to front for trust companies, without being able or willing to provide the high staffing requirement and degree of computerization which may be thought desirable in the interests of effective management. Any practitioner advising in relation to a time-share project should make inquiries as to these matters.

Flexibility
The club/trustee system is adaptable. In jurisdictions which do not recognize trusts, the assets can be trans-

ferred to a corporation incorporated in a jurisdiction which does recognize trusts, and the shares, as opposed to the property, vested in trust. If, as in Malta and certain parts of Greece, local law prevents acquisition of real property by foreign nationals, the rights can be secured by mortgage granted in favor of the trustee or its nominee, instead of a transfer of the title of the property itself.

Floating units, where the member has a right of occupation of a particular type of unit, as opposed to a specific unit, can also be created. The time-share right, once created, is easily transferable (most membership certificates have a form of transfer endorsed on the back of the certificate). The system lends itself to combination with escrow provisions, and the use of the certificate as security is easily achieved without cumbersome formality. Sales can be made in a chosen jurisdiction by using applications for membership to be accepted in that jurisdiction, and combining this with management and promotional services agreements. This may have important tax and exchange control advantages. The transaction can be consummated quickly, and without burdensome registration formalities. The trustee can in fact operate the membership registry. The cost per sale is much less in a club/trustee system than in a system which relies for its effectiveness on the registration of a freehold or leasehold interest in a public registry.

The formalities on involuntary devolution are less onerous (for example, there is usually no need to obtain a grant of administration in a foreign jurisdiction). These advantages seem certain to secure an important role for the club/trustee system in the international development of time-sharing, particularly in view of the recent Hague Convention provision for overseas recognition of United Kingdom trusts. There is no doubt, however, that legislation is urgently needed to combat abuse of the system, to establish the minimum qualification of trustees and mandatory requirements as to the provisions to be incorporated in the club/trustee documentation. The rules of the European Holiday Timeshare Association are a good indication as to what is required in this respect, and their regulations regarding trustees were derived from the Banking Act 1979 (licensing deposit takers) and the Public Trustee Rules 1911 (as amended).

Six Steps to Reading the Report

Step One: Recall: What Do You Know About Time-Sharing?

You buy a flat or apartment for, say, only four weeks of the year, for your own occupancy. All the other weeks of the year are owned by other people, who occupy it on a similar basis. Usually this type of accommodation is abroad. Legally there are all sorts of problems. It is important to check on the soundness of the financial and legal basis of the development. Many people have lost all their money in time-share ventures. Then who is responsible for managing the flat and the whole complex? Check legal, administrative, financial, and maintenance management.

Step Two: Objectives: Why Are You Reading This Report?

Having glanced through the article and spotted the subheading Consumer Protection:

- You want to be able to recognize an honest club system.

- What differences are there between the laws of England and other countries relating to this subject?

Remember that some objectives may not be answered by this document.

Step Three: Overview

Note in the introduction (italics) that this is the third part of a five-part series and not the last, so there is no conclusion here today. The scheme is in operation in the United Kingdom and the Mediterranean countries. There are three subheadings: Documentation, Consumer Protection, and Flexibility. Under Consumer Protection, paragraphs are clearly defined.

Step Four: Preview

Keeping your objectives firmly in mind, reject whatever does not respond to them. This includes the first two paragraphs above the subheading Documentation; under Flexibility, all you need to know is that the system is adaptable, so the rest seems irrelevant to your immediate concern.

Step Five: Inview

Now read steadily, with a rhythm. The columns are narrow, the vocabulary familiar, so you should need only one fixation per line. But read each line: You want comprehension. If you feel you are going too fast, slow down, but do not regress.

Read with a pencil or highlighter and mark the keywords that answer your objectives.

The documentation is made up of four sections describing:

■ An association held together by a set of rules;

■ A management agreement that defines the distribution of running costs between members;

■ A trust deed to safeguard assets of the members; and

■ A sales contract identifying parties, time, and unit involved.

A club system has two essential advantages:

■ Consumer protection.

■ Flexibility

It hinges on the trustee, an independent body. The trustee is responsible for the running costs of the units, so that if the promoter is bankrupt, dishonest, or has ordinary cash-flow problems, the members keep their right to their properties. It means that moneys are under the control of the trustee, that records are kept by him or her, and that moneys are invested, or used appropriately. Anyone thinking of a time-share abroad should inquire about the total independence of the trustee, as promoters have been known to use "off-the-shelf" companies to their own benefit rather than that of their clients.

Step Six: Review

On reviewing the objectives, the answers, and the report, you may notice that there is some information under the heading Flexibility that is interesting in its own right. So you may adopt a flexible approach and re-inview some of those paragraphs originally rejected. You probably will not be much clearer about the differences between English and other countries' laws and will seek more information elsewhere.

Having got many of the answers to your objectives, here is a recall pattern (see Figure 6.1).

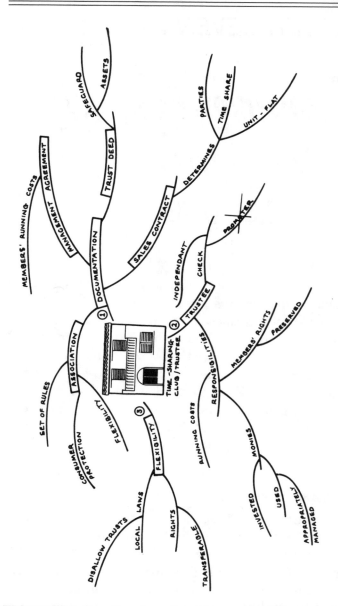

FIGURE 6.1 Recall pattern for notes on time-sharing—the club/ trustee system.

Crossing out a note lightly indicates that this note is a situation that is wrong.

CHAPTER SEVEN

Applying Rapid Reading to Newspapers, Journals, and Meetings

In this chapter . . .

Newspapers, journals, and similar documents lend themselves well to rapid reading. The method is simplified, as you need only a few of the six steps.

Meetings can be modeled on a streamlined systematic approach to reading:

■ Objectives and Overview.

- Preview and Inview simultaneously.

- Review.

This chapter concludes by wishing you well on your journal of continuous discovery of knowledge.

Newspapers

Newspapers are divided into sections—home and international news, entertainment and arts reviews, sports, medical reports, business news, advertisements, and so on. If you buy the same newspaper every day, you become familiar with its presentation and style. Over the months, or years, you practice Overviewing your newspaper, and you know where to find the type of information you are seeking. What changes every day, though, is the content.

As you move to a page that interests you, say, international news, you should skim over it, noting headlines and selecting mentally those articles that you wish to read. When you are ready to read, a newspaper gives you an advantage over other printed material to practice conditioning: Its narrow columns make it easy to have one fixation per line—perhaps even one per paragraph. You can go very fast.

A news article is constructed so that the most important information is contained in the opening paragraphs; the rest is detail or reinforcement. Apply Previewing, paying attention to the beginning and exercising the art of rejection. Remember that a newspaper either summarizes what happened yesterday or anticipates what may happen tomorrow. If you buy a newspaper or listen to the news every day, you have a lot of background information, and thus can dispense with most of the six systematic steps.

Let us consider an article from the *Times* (London).

Pöhl Walks Tightrope
of German Consensus

It is inconceivable in today's Britain that Robin Leigh-Pemberton would be reappointed Governor of the Bank of England had Mrs. Thatcher lost the election. Indeed, his original appointment, before the 1983 election, proved so politically controversial that Labour would have pushed him out straight away had it won then. Luckily for the Germans, things are ordered differently in Bonn, where almost everyone is in favour of a monetary policy that will not permit rampant inflation. It was thus almost a formality that Karl Otto Pöhl gained a further eight-year term as President of the Bundesbank, though he was once as closely associated with the opposition Social Democrats, who appointed him, as Mr. Leigh-Pemberton was with the Conservative Party.

Performance may also have something to do with it. The Governor is by no means certain of another term next year, since he has not always shown a safe pair of hands. Herr Pöhl, by contrast, has emerged as one of the two most influential central bankers in international discussion of exchange rate and monetary cooperation. Since the other, Paul Volcker, is on the way out, Herr Pöhl is likely to be called on for leadership.

He will not be giving an unequivocal message. The Bundesbank has recently used an exchange rate target for monetary policy almost as much as the Treasury and the Bank of England and has likewise exceeded its targets for monetary growth. There are two differences. West Germany still has negligible inflation, mainly thanks to the improving terms of trade—though this could change if dollar weakness persists into a period of rising commodity prices. And, as Herr Pöhl made clear yesterday, the Bundesbank feels guilty about exceeding monetary targets, while the British authorities prefer to pretend nothing is amiss.

The great strength of German monetary policy, however, is the overt restriction on its scope. Monetary targets are set to accommodate the expected trends in the economy without inflation (or deflation). They are not used, as in Britain, or especially the United States, as a principal lever on the economy. The reluctance of the Germans to engage in a positive policy of cutting interest rates to stimulate their sluggish economy is, for this reason, often misinterpreted as excessive caution.

The continuing message from Herr Pöhl will surely be that less weight be placed on monetary management as a policy tool. Fiscal policy is to stimulate or rein back demand and direct action should be used to help stabilize exchange rates within that framework. In that context, Herr Pöhl has proved a constant and persuasive lobbyist for sterling to be fixed to the EMS.

German monetary policy has worked partly because history has produced a consensus fearful of inflation but also because the independent central bank has not been obliged, like Mr. Volcker, to bear too much of the burden of economic management. This is an important message for Herr Pöhl to evangelize, not least at home where his opposite number, the finance minister Gerhard Stoltenburg, despite the supposedly close working relationship between the two, has not been as adventurous as he might have been in cutting taxes, liberalizing the economy and boosting domestic demand to replace exports.

This article illustrates the nature of newspaper material. The opening paragraph compares the heads of Britain's and Germany's central banks, bringing the reader quickly into perspective; it sets the scene.

The second, third, and fourth paragraphs refresh the reader's mind about inflation in Germany and the German position on monetary policy. It does not impart any new knowledge.

The last two paragraphs open up new ideas:

1. The desire of the Germans to have sterling within the EMS;

2. The possible strategies Herr Pöhl and the Finance Minister can use in order to boost the German economy.

If you usually keep an eye on European economic affairs, you need to read the first and last two paragraphs only.

Journals

The main trouble with journals is the frequency with which they appear in your in-tray. Journals are aimed at a professional body but, within this, include a variety of subjects aimed at reaching all their readership with at least one article per issue. Overview the whole journal by looking at the table of contents. Note the article or articles you may want to read. Preview by turning to the appropriate pages and then locate and read the synopsis and conclusion. If there are none, read the opening and concluding paragraphs. If you decide you need more information, read the rest, using the conditioning approach, looking for key ideas and using a guide.

If you own the copy of the journal and are not interested in the advertising, tear it apart so that you save only the article(s) you need.

Let us take as an example an article from *Forbes* magazine.

Talking Tough
by Howard Banks

Created with $10 billion in government subsidies, Airbus Industrie seems able to stand on its own feet. Be warned, Boeing.

Typical of the Continent on the eve of 1992, Airbus Industrie, the European civil airliner consortium, is bursting with confidence. Orders it has already taken will ensure that by 1993–94 it will deliver a 40% world share of all wide-body airliners. An 800-aircraft backlog puts it on track to grab the 30% share of the world jet airliner market that was the original aim of the founders of the European project, 21 years ago.

The giant in the business, Seattle-based Boeing, most recently has felt forced to launch its new twin-engined airliner, the 777, to compete with the market success of the Airbus A330. Since Boeing has 60% of the world jet market and Airbus is on its way to 30%, there are slim pickings for the rest, most notably hard-pressed McDonnell Douglas.

The market has become so strong that Airbus has shaken off its traditional price discounting and has been slowly pushing up prices on its aircraft. Says Airbus' newly reappointed managing director, Jean Pierson, 49, "The consortium should be operating in the black by the end of 1993."

Pierson smiles. He is, of course, not counting the billions—maybe as much as $10 billion—that the European governments have sunk into developing the company and its products. This was pure subsidy, in the beginning a highly political make-work program frankly intended to reclaim part of the jet airliner business from the Americans. Pierson is talking only about operating profit, covering the cost of current production.

Nevertheless, Airbus is finally close to standing on its own. It now offers a full range of aircraft, modeled after Boeing's "family" concept. Airbus airliners start with the 150-seat, single-aisle, short-to-medium-range A320. Next comes a series of short-to-long-range, twin-aisle, twin-engine types carrying from 210 to 385 passengers up to 5,000 miles. Finally, scheduled to fly in 1992 is a very long-range (8,500 miles) four-engine A340.

The consortium's newfound strength and competitiveness reflect a new feistiness on the part of the European companies that are partners in Airbus. West Germany's MBB, with a 37.9% share, is now owned by private-sector Daimler-Benz. British Aerospace (20% share) was privatized in 1981 and is turning into a highly aggressive company. Even French state-owned Aérospatiale (37.9% share) is now embarked on its own toughening up and cost-cutting drive and is talking of selling part of its equity to its workers. (CASA of Spain has the remaining 4.2% stake in Airbus Industrie.)

One result of all this is that development money for new Airbus programs no longer depends on government handouts. The $500 million upfront cost of the stretched A321 now in development was, for instance, raised by the partners on their own. Last month the European Community, bowing to U.S. pressure in the GATT negotiations over aircraft subsidies, offered to end production subsidies for Airbus.

The latter isn't much of a concession, considering that Airbus probably no longer is in such need of the handouts. It has just ridden out a four-month strike at the British Aerospace plant that makes the wings for all Airbuses. This cut planned deliveries in 1989 from 138 aircraft to 105 and, says Jean Pierson, cost the company $180 million to $200 million in operating profit. It was a strike the company could ill afford in the past. When it ended, Airbus announced that it is increasing production rates to around 180 a year, an alltime high, and that deliveries should be back to normal some time in 1991.

Airbus is also taking unusually calmly the publicly announced plans of Indian Airlines, following a crash, to dump its existing fleet of A320s. The crash, it seems from initial investigations, was caused by pilot error. But quiet sniping from U.S. sources hints that the complexity of the so-called fly-by-wire cockpit system of the A320 might have contributed. (In a fly-by-wire system the pilots control the aircraft via computers, instead of directly through pulleys and wires that actuate hydraulic rams on the aircraft's control surfaces on the wings and tail plane.) Boeing has chosen a different version of this technology for its new 777.

The Airbus fly-by-wire cockpit is an example of Airbus' willingness to push the latest technology further than its U.S. rivals. This willingness has also produced a new modular assembly technique, which Airbus claims is more efficient. It is to be used to build two new related planes, the twin-engine A330 and the four-engine A340, on a common assembly line, where most of the detailed work will be done in a dock, with the aircraft stationary. This breaks with the conventional Henry Ford-like system, where the aircraft moves down the line at each stage of assembly.

The major plane components—the wings, fuselage sections and tail surfaces—are made in the partners' factories and shipped by air to Toulouse. In a much more automated process than is common today, the major elements of the aircraft will be bolted together into a plane that can be moved on its own wheels, though without engines. The plane will then proceed to a nearby bay, where it will stay until all system tests and the remaining structural assembly have been completed. The workers will move to the plane, rather than the other way around. And they will work on either type, interchangeably.

This innovative process has three key results: It cuts the assembly cycle time by about 20 % ; it increases manufacturing flexibility, and, finally, as a consequence cuts the cost of the final aircraft. The new assembly line, for instance, allows changes much later in production—between the two types of aircraft, the A330 and A340, as well as between the widely different interiors required by different airlines—than on a conventional line. "We are not Boeing. They are so big they can resist airline pressure for late changes. We cannot," says Claude Terrazzoni, executive vice president of Aérospatiale, which spearheaded the new manufacturing technique.

The next major step, Pierson says, will be to change the corporate structure, to make Airbus more like a normal company better able to attract private investment capital on its own. It was born, for instance, as a peculiar French creation, called a Groupement Intérêt Economique, which has insulated it from normal requirements such as publishing any kind of financial statements. There are problems converting it to a normal public limited company, though, explains Pierson, however attractive that might be in theory. Airbus itself owns none of the assets, the factories or the machine tools used to produce its planes. They belong to the partners and, in many cases, are not used exclusively for the Airbus program.

One possibility, however, might eventually be to issue stock in Airbus, with a majority going to the partners according to their share of the program. The remainder could be sold, to workers and on the market. Pierson thinks that would open Airbus accounts to greater scrutiny and that it could lead to much more open—and competitive—bidding for work between the partners, instead of the work allocation that now occurs.

Would Airbus stock be a good investment? Much, of course, depends on the price, but it has its potential appeal. A massive market for civilian airliners exists. Airbus has technology as good as its American rivals' and is being run by a new generation of combative bosses. Typical is Richard Evans, 48, chief executive of partner British Aerospace, who says: "Airbus is going to attack the Americans, including Boeing, until they bleed and scream. And we are going to make a lot of money in the process." Its executives wouldn't have talked that way a half-decade ago.

Applying rapid reading to this article:

1. What do you know?

Airbus is a recently developed European commercial aircraft. It was financed through government subsidies. It is now taking some of the world market share.

2. Set objectives.

You want to learn how Airbus has become an aggressive competitor. You also want to learn if Boeing is retaliating, and if so, how.

3. Overview.

Zigzagging down the columns, you may note that the article describes

- The makeup of the consortium.
- The new financing arrangements.
- Past problems—a strike that affected the production line and the highly computerized system that became a concern when an Airbus crashed.
- The highly automated assembly.
- The future, as seen by the chief executive of Airbus.

Thus, the article does not seem to contain much useful information about your second objective, whether Boeing is retaliating.

4. Preview and inview (combine them for this example).

The first paragraph imparts important information that you may read with care—using a cruising speed—and you note that by 1993 to 1994 Airbus Industrie will have taken 30 percent of the market share. You then may read the second paragraph at the same speed, learning that Boeing is competing with a new twin-engined plane.

The third, fourth, and fifth paragraphs also contribute toward your objectives, so you may continue to cruise. You would take in that discount policy is being dropped, that the company will be in the black, and that Airbus has modeled itself on Boeing by producing a "family" of planes.

The next four paragraphs do not address your objectives directly, so you would skim over them. However, you might slow down again toward the end of the article, as it explains clearly why Airbus Industrie is becoming competitive. The end focuses on the automation process that allows for changes late in production, the planned change in company infrastructure to attract private investment, and the possibility of issuing stock to raise capital.

5. Review

Make a recall pattern for notes (see Figure 7.1).

Meetings

You can handle a meeting the same way you handle a book. All you need to do is change the technique terminology.

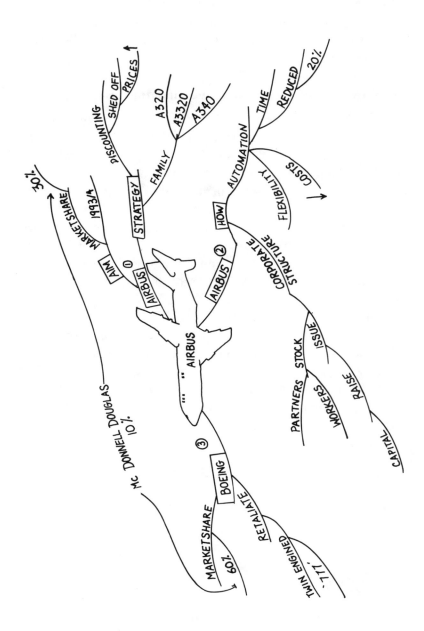

FIGURE 7.1 Recall pattern for Airbus Industrie article.

Normally, when you are asked to a meeting you know why—you know the parameters. That is what an agenda is for—the objectives. If you do not have agendas, your office may need to review the way it organizes meetings. In this case, you can jot down, using a recall pattern, the possible issues to be discussed. This is your overview.

As you listen to the information, you use previewing and inviewing simultaneously. The previewing allows you to connect ideas quickly, and inviewing occurs when you question the speaker on a point of particular interest. To keep your concentration and for future reference, make notes. Using recall patterns makes it easier, as you were given the structure with the agenda. Also new information, questions, and corrections can be added easily to the pattern notes.

After the meeting, review the notes to reinforce your long-term memory and fill your knowledge gaps. Pick up any outstanding points that need to be followed up later.

Conclusion

The key objectives this book set out to achieve were to give you:

- Confidence.
- Technique.
- Flexibility.

If you have improved your reading speed and comprehension, you can maintain and improve them further. Regular practice is the key to keeping and improving a newly acquired skill. As you become more familiar with the technique, you can, of course, tailor it to your own style and requirements.

Some readers will have found each step easy to absorb and apply, others will not. If you found the steps difficult, mastering them is a matter of perseverance. Repeat each step until it becomes second nature.

Rapid reading expands your capacity to concentrate, sharpens your memory, and permits you to widen your interests. There is no limit to your latent talents. This book is only the beginning—go out and tackle other areas of knowledge and interest. Good luck!

Bibliography

The Brain

Brown, Mark. *Left Handed: Right Handed.* Newton Abbot: David and Charles.

Hunt, Morton. *The Universe Within.* London: Corgi.

Luria, A. R. *The Working Brain.* New York: Basic Books.

Russell, Peter. *The Brain Book.* New York: Dutton.

Searleman, A. "A review of right hemisphere linguistic capabilities." *Psychological Bulletin* 84, no. 3.

Smith, Anthony. *The Mind.* New York: Penguin.

Winter, Arthur, M.D., and Ruth Winter. *Build Your Brain Power.* New York: St. Martin's Press.

Young, J. Z. *Programs of the Brain.* Oxford: Oxford University Press.

Dyslexia

Augur, Jean. *This Book Doesn't Make Sense.*

Hornsby, B. *Overcoming Dyslexia.* Kinderhook, NY: E. J. Brill.

McAuslan, Alan. *Dyslexia: What Parents Ought to Know.* London: Penguin.

National Institute of Dyslexia
3200 Woodbine Street
Chevy Chase, MD 20815

Orton Dyslexia Society
724 York Road
Baltimore, MD 21204

Eyes

Bates, W. H. *The Bates Method for Better Eyesight Without Glasses*. Fort Worth: Holt, Rinehart and Winston.

Huxley, A. *The Art of Seeing*. Creative Arts Books.

Reading

Agardy, F. J. "How to read faster and better." *Evelyn Wood in Reading Dynamics*. New York: Simon & Schuster.

Buzan, Tony. *Speed Reading*. New York: Dutton.

―――. *Use Your Head*. London: Ariel Publications.

Fink, Diane D., et al. Speedreading: *The How-to Book for Every Busy Manager, Executive and Professional*. New York: Wiley.

References

Banks, Howard, "Talking Tough." *Forbes* Magazine, 23 July 1990.

Barzini, Luigi. *The Europeans*. New York: Penguin.

Edmonds, James. "Time-Sharing—the club/trustee system." *The Law Society's Gazette*, 7 Jan. 1987.

Kipling, Rudyard. *I Keep Six Honest Serving-Men*.

Luria, A. R. *The Mind of a Mnemonist*. Cambridge: Harvard University Press.

"Pöhl walks tightrope of German consensus." *The Times* (London), 25 June 1987.

Stuart, Cristina. *How to Be an Effective Speaker*. Lincolnwood, IL: NTC Business Books.

Toffler, Alvin. *Future Shock*. New York: Random House.

Index

About the Author ════

Kathryn Redway was born and educated in France, where she was graduated with degrees in languages and philosophy. After several years of practical business experience in the United States and in Europe, she specialized in creating workshops and seminars for personal development.

Redway has lectured extensively in the United Kingdom and in Europe. One of her principal activities has been working with industrial clients to develop company programs of management techniques, including communication, creativity, and managing change and innovation. She has also worked with multinational companies in solving problems of internal communication and in establishing goals.

Redway has written extensively about her work and has appeared on television to discuss it.

Among her current clients are international companies in oil, electronics, construction, aviation, and food as well as government agencies and university departments.